佛教英语交流基地系列丛书◎ 明生 主编

六祖坛经

（元）宗宝编◎来东 潘远梦 池濂 等译

THE PLATFORM SUTRA OF THE SIXTH PATRIARCH

Edited by Zong Bao (Yuan Dynasty)
Translated by Laidong Pan Yuan Meng Chi Lian et al

宗教文化出版社

图书在版编目（CIP）数据

六祖坛经 = The Platform Sutra of the Sixth Patriarch : 汉、英 / (元) 宗宝编 ; 来东等译 . -- 北京 : 宗教文化出版社 , 2023.12

（佛教英语交流基地系列丛书）

ISBN 978-7-5188-1546-3

Ⅰ . ①六… Ⅱ . ①宗… ②来… Ⅲ . ①《六祖坛经》—汉、英 Ⅳ . ① B946.5

中国国家版本馆 CIP 数据核字 (2024) 第 014231 号

六祖坛经

The Platform Sutra of the Sixth Patriarch

（元）宗宝 编　来东、潘远梦、池濂等 译

出版发行：宗教文化出版社

地　　址：北京市西城区后海北沿 44 号（100009）

电　　话：64095215（发行部）　64095265（编辑部）

责任编辑：王志宏

封面设计：明　齐　陶映琳

版式设计：武俊东

印　　刷：河北信瑞彩印刷有限公司

版本记录：880 毫米 ×1230 毫米　32 开　5.5 印张　200 千字

2024 年 10 月第 1 版　2024 年 10 月第 1 次印刷

书　　号：ISBN 978-7-5188-1546-3

定　　价：88.00 元

佛教英语交流基地系列丛书项目组

Translation Project of the Series of English Base for Buddhist Exchange

目　录
Contents

序　言

2017 年 6 月，在四众护持和多方努力下，佛教英语交流基地在珠海普陀寺成立。普陀寺风景之秀，佛法之隆，人才之众，为伽蓝之冠。基地借此天时地利人和之便，发展迅速，欣欣向荣。基地成立的初衷是为了更好地继承和发扬中华民族优秀的传统文化，在促进文化交流，提高文化自信的同时，服务于新时代中国特色社会主义的建设。而佛教作为中华文化的重要组成部分，在新的历史时代，也面临着推陈出新、去芜存菁的挑战。基地立足于禅宗祖庭，在讲好"中国佛教故事"，加速佛教中国化的进程上，进行了很多有益的尝试，积累了丰富的经验，也取得了不错的成果。其中一个重要且有益的成果就是眼前这本由佛教英语交流基地的僧才翻译的中英双语《六祖坛经》。

选择《六祖坛经》作为译介的第一部佛教典籍，背后的用意是十分明显的。太虚大师讲"中国佛学的特质在禅"，发扬禅宗就是发扬中国化的佛教，而禅宗的典籍中最重要的便是这部《六祖坛经》。中国的佛教典籍洋洋洒洒，但唯一能称得上是经的只此一部。《六祖坛经》不光在语言上通俗易懂，内容上也强调"明心见性""不立文字""顿悟成佛"等教外别传的见解；其中的许多故事、偈颂都演为后世的公案话头，而六祖禅语中的机敏和锋芒，恰恰是中华文化中最有活性的部分。

关于《六祖坛经》的译本，已经有很多了，最早的可以追溯到黄茂林的译本，晚近台湾佛学界也翻译不少，譬如成观法师以及佛教徒林光明、蔡坤昌和林怡馨先后都有译本。基地翻译的底本是元代宗宝所编的《六祖大师法宝坛经》。比起学术价值，更看重这个版本的流通性。虽然翻译是在语言文字上下功夫，但字句上用了太多功夫，反倒耽误禅宗的精神，最后译本不免沦为案头的作品。基地的翻译重在“去形存神”，用贴近生活的语言传译，尽可能保留禅宗语录的口头语体色彩。另外，尽可能保留佛教的名相，而不是化用西方的哲学概念去解释禅宗思想。在偈颂的翻译上，运用无韵的句子去翻译，保证偈颂形式的同时，古典中文的韵律自然丢失不少。《六祖坛经》中讲：“人有南北，法无顿渐。”正因为人有南北，语言也有南北。中英双语，本不同根，翻译之上，难免顾此失彼。除此之外，南禅又是活禅，不是枯禅、寒禅，慧能的语言自然也是活的。活的语言是很难翻译的，将《六祖坛经》中灵活利落的禅机传播万一，已非易事；至于错误和不足之处，在所难免，还请方家指正。

多年前，世界佛学研究以梵文巴利文的典籍为主。现在潮流变了，随着中国的国际地位提高，世界人民对中国文化的兴趣也提高了。汉传大乘佛教，尤其是禅宗思想渐趋流行。越来越多的人开始关注禅文化，想要了解禅文化。和吉光片羽的梵文贝叶不同，禅宗一花五叶，枝繁叶茂，留下的灯谱语录，数不胜数，怎么把其中的精华介绍给大家就成了一个问题。但这问题不难解决——佛教是怎么借着译经僧的笔传入华夏的就怎么传出。而翻译可以说是文化传播的不二法门。我相信佛教英语交流基地在这方面是走在前面的。

之所以要传播禅文化，是因为中国禅文化是大乘佛教，大乘佛教不光自度还要度人。所以不论是讲好中国故事还是加速佛教中国化进程，不论是向内还是向外，目的只有一个——把大乘的菩提思想和般若智慧传播到群众中去，让大家都“见自本心”，识得“本来面目”。但是仅凭借语言文字是不行的，必须现身说法，因此必须培养人才，运用人才。不光社会发展需要人才，文化传播也需要，这部双语的《坛经》就是人才的劳动成果。所以基地在之后的建设中，要培养更多的人才，给人才更多的展示空间。让基地成为佛教界语言人才的摇篮。

关于这部《六祖坛经》翻译更为殊胜的地方在于，该书是基地僧才在千年祖庭光孝禅寺翻译完成的。千年前，六祖在光孝垂范传灯，留《六祖坛经》一部，而后衍为禅门五家七宗之盛。千年后，六祖遗训又于祖庭之中被翻译为外语，传播到远方，不能不说是汉传佛教史的一件大事。其中的护法之情，千载而遥，精气相通。在此我代表广东佛教界，向佛教英语交流基地的僧才，表达我的感谢之情。感谢他们为大乘佛法的传播做出的贡献。虽然这贡献还并不大，但是，涓滴之念，功不唐捐，默默积累，终成菩提。在他们身上，我还看到新时代僧人应有的使命和担当。除此之外，希望他们继续发扬佛教僧人的研学译经的风气，翻译出更多更好的作品，以飨读者；在向外传播的同时，加速佛教中国化的进程，为新时代祖国的文化发展，贡献自己的力量。

明生

2024 年 3 月

Preface

In June 2017, with the support of the local Buddhist community and the efforts of different parties, the English Base for Buddhist Exchange (EBBE) was established in Zhuhai Putuo Temple. Taking advantage of the temple's beautiful scenery, flourishing Dharma and talents, the EBBE develops rapidly and prospers. The original purpose of the EBBE is to inherit and carry forward the fine Chinese traditional culture so as to promote cultural exchanges, enhance cultural confidence, and serve the construction of Chinese socialism in the new era. As an integral part of Chinese culture, Buddhism is also facing the challenge of innovation and adaptation in the new era. Located in a temple belonging to the Chan school, the EBBE has made a lot of useful attempts to foster the localization of Buddhism and bring Chan teachings to the global stage. Throughout this journey, the EBBE has gained significant experience and accomplished commendable achievements. One of the achievements is the bilingual *Platform Sutra* translated by talents from the EBBE.

The decision to translate the *Platform Sutra* as the first Buddhist classic is no coincidence. As Master Taixu once said, "Chinese Buddhism is characterized by Chan". Thus, to promote Chan is to promote Chinese Buddhism. The most important Chan text is the *Platform Sutra*. In the sea of Buddhist texts authored by Chinese masters, this is the only one that truly merits the title of a sutra. This sutra features an easy-to-understand language and offers unique insights such as "purifying the mind and seeing the nature," "not clinging to words," and "achieving sudden enlightenment," etc. Many of its stories and poems have become the subject of discussion for later generations. The wit and discernment demonstrated in the master's teachings unveil the most vibrant facets of Chinese culture.

Among the many translations of the *Platform Sutra*, the earliest version was done by Huang Maolin, and recent translations were mainly contributed by talents or monastics from Taiwan, such as Venerable Chengguan, and lay Buddhists Lin Guangming, Cai Kunchang and Lin Yixin. The translation you see before you is based on the *Dharma Treasure Platform Sutra of the Sixth Patriarch* compiled by Master Zongbao in the Yuan dynasty. We value this text more for its wide circulation rather than its research value. Although translation is a craft performed on the linguistic level, in this case, a literal and strictly academic translation will erode the spirit of Chan and end up on the desk, collecting dust. Using daily expressions to preserve as much as possible the oral and stylistic nuances of Chan discourse, this translation tries to "retain the spirit and forsake the form". In addition, we try to use the original Buddhist terms as much as possible, instead of applying Western philosophical concepts to approximate Chan thought. In translating Buddhist verses, plain sentences were used, which might impair the rhyme inherent in classical Chinese. But this option is justified by the difference between Chinese and English languages as well as the essence of Chan Buddhism. The *Platform Sutra* says, "There is only one Dharma despite the differences among people". Different people are represented by different languages. Due to the vast difference between Chinese and English, translation inevitably involves some compromise in form for the sake of content. In addition, the Southern Chan school is marked by its dynamism instead of rigidity; so is Hui Neng's discourse. All these difficulties make mistakes inevitable, and we welcome your critiques and corrections.

Many years ago, the study of Buddhism in the world was dominated by Sanskrit and Pali texts. Now the trend has changed. With the rising international status of China, the world's interest in Chinese culture has also surged. Chinese Mahayana Buddhism, especially the teaching of the Chan school, is gaining popularity. A growing number of people have shifted their attention to Chan culture and show keen curiosity about this ancient wisdom. Unlike the sparse Pattra-leaf scriptures, Chan school, with its five branches, left with the world countless discourses and stories. This treasure trove poses a challenge on how to introduce them. But this is not difficult to solve – we simply translate them in the way ancient monks translated the Sanskrit scriptures. In fact, translation is indispensable to cultural transmission. I believe that the EBBE is at the forefront of this significant endeavor.

Belonging to Mahayana Buddhism, which commands its disciples to liberate both themselves and others, the Chan school makes transmission of the teaching its responsibility. Transmitting Buddhism, whether domestically or internationally, aims to spread the compassion and wisdom of Mahayana Buddhism so that all of us can "see the Intrinsic Nature". However, mere language and text are insufficient. Cultural transmission relies heavily on the intellectual resource, so it is necessary to cultivate Buddhist talents who can meet the demand for social development and cultural dissemination. In fact, this bilingual *Platform Sutra* is a testament to the dedication and endeavour of the talents who work on it. In its subsequent construction, the EBBE will continue to establish itself as a cradle of linguistic talents and a platform for Buddhist cultural exchanges.

What is even more remarkable about this bilingual *Platform Sutra* is that it was completed in Guangxiao Temple, the thousand-year-old cradle of Chan Buddhism. Thousands of years ago, the Sixth Patriarch gave his teaching here, the origin of all the later seven Chan schools. Today, his legacy was translated into a foreign language and spread worldwide, marking a significant milestone in the history of Chinese Buddhism. The resolve to protect the Dharma remains as strong as it was thousands of years ago. On behalf of the Guangdong Buddhist Community, I would like to express my gratitude to the talents from the EBBE for their contribution to the spread of Mahayana Buddhism. Although their contribution might seem modest now, the accumulation of efforts will eventually lead them to enlightenment. In their dedication, I also see the mission and responsibility that monks should embrace in the new era. I hope that they persist in their studies and translation so as to produce more and better translations for readers. While they make an effort to transmit Buddhism to the world, I hope they will make a unique contribution to Chinese Buddhism by accelerating the localization of Buddhism.

明生

March, 2024

行由品第一
Chapter 1 Autobiography

时，大师至宝林，韶州韦刺史与官僚入山，请师出。于城中大梵寺讲堂，为众开缘说法。师升座次，刺史官僚三十余人，儒宗学士三十余人，僧尼道俗一千余人，同时作礼，愿闻法要。

Once, upon the great Master's arrival at the Baolin Temple, Prefect Wei of Shaozhou together with other officials visited the monastery and invited him to teach Dharma publicly at the lecture hall of the Dafan Temple in town. After the Master was seated, his guests, more than thirty officials, thirty Confucians and one thousand monastics and lay people, paid homage to him and requested him to teach the essentials of Dharma.

大师告众曰：善知识！菩提自性，本来清净，但用此心，直了成佛。善知识！且听惠能行由得法事意。

The Master instructed, "My Dharma friends, our Intrinsic Nature is pure by essence. Rely on it, and you'll directly get enlightened and attain Buddhahood. My Dharma friends, please allow me to tell you how I obtained Dharma.

惠能严父，本贯范阳。左降流于岭南，作新州百姓；此身不幸，父又早亡，老母孤遗，移来南海，艰辛贫乏，于市卖柴。时，有一客买柴，使令送至客店；客收去，惠能得钱，却出门外，见一客诵经。惠能一闻经语，心即开悟，遂问：客诵何经？客曰：《金刚经》。复问：从何所来，持此经典？客云：我从蕲州黄梅县东禅寺来。其寺是五祖忍大师在彼主化，门人一千有余；我到彼中礼拜，听受此经。大师常劝僧俗：但持《金刚经》，即自见性，直了成佛。

"My father, a native of Fanyang County, was deprived of his official status and banished to Xinzhou, Lingnan as a mere commoner. Unfortunately, he passed away when I was young, leaving my mother and me in a dire situation. Impoverished, we moved to Nanhai and made a living by collecting and selling firewood. One day, someone bought my firewood and asked me to send it to his shop. I went to the shop and was paid there. Just as I was about to leave, I saw a customer chanting a sutra. On hearing it, I was suddenly enlightened. So I asked him what sutra he was chanting. He said, '*The Diamond Sutra*'. I then asked him where he was from and how he got this sutra. He replied, 'I came from the Dongchan Temple in Huangmei, Qizhou. The Fifth Patriarch Master Hongren presides there with more than one thousand followers. I paid a visit there and received the teachings on this sutra. He often advised monastics and the laity to chant *The Diamond Sutra*, which would lead directly to your Intrinsic Nature and Buddhahood.'

惠能闻说，宿昔有缘，乃蒙一客，取银十两与惠能，令充老母衣粮，教便往黄梅参礼五祖。惠能安置母毕，即便辞违。不经三十余日，便至黄梅，礼拜五祖。

“After hearing this, [I decided to visit him.] Luckily, another customer, who may be karmically connected to me, sponsored my trip and my mother's livelihood. After making a proper arrangement for my mother, I took my leave. In less than thirty days, I arrived in Huangmei and paid homage to the Patriarch.

祖问曰：汝何方人？欲求何物？

“The Patriarch then asked, ‘Where are you from and what do you want from me?’

惠能对曰：弟子是岭南新州百姓，远来礼师，惟求作佛，不求余物。

“I replied, ‘I am a commoner from Xinzhou in Lingnan. I came all this way for nothing but the attainment of Buddhahood.’

祖言：汝是岭南人，又是獦獠，若为堪作佛？

“He said, ‘How can you, a barbarian from Lingnan, expect to attain Buddhahood?’

惠能曰：人虽有南北，佛性本无南北；獦獠身与和尚不同，佛性有何差别？

“I replied, ‘The Buddha Nature has nothing to do with where a man is from, be it the South or the North. A barbarian and your Most Venerable may differ in appearance, but not in Buddha Nature.’

五祖更欲与语，且见徒众总在左右，乃令随众作务。

"Despite his willingness to carry on the dialogue, he restrained it, due to the presence of his disciples, and ordered me to join the group in monastic chores instead.

惠能曰：惠能启和尚，弟子自心，常生智慧，不离自性，即是福田。未审和尚教作何务？
"But I continued, 'Most Venerable, I'd like to tell you that wisdom often arises in my mind which never deviates from Intrinsic Nature, and this is exactly the state that produces merit for spiritual practice, so I am wondering what the point is.'

祖云：这獦獠根性大利，汝更勿言，着槽厂去。
"The Fifth Patriarch thought, 'This barbarian has a really sharp faculty for Dharma!' He stopped me and said, 'Say no more! Go to work in the backyard.'

惠能退至后院，有一行者，差惠能破柴踏碓。经八月余，祖一日忽见惠能曰：吾思汝之见可用，恐有恶人害汝，遂不与汝言，汝知之否？惠能曰：弟子亦知师意，不敢行至堂前，令人不觉。
"Then I went there, and a monastic member ordered me to split the firewood and mill the rice. About eight months later, the Fifth Patriarch suddenly came to me and said, 'I didn't acknowledge your words back then, which were insightful, because I feared that some villains might do you harm. Did you know my intention at that time?' I replied, 'Yes, I knew. That's why I didn't dare to approach you lest I should attract attention.'

祖一日唤诸门人总来。吾向汝说：世人生死事大。汝等终日只求福田，不求出离生死苦海。自性若迷，福何可救？汝等各去自看智慧，取自本心般若之性，各作一偈，来呈吾看。若悟大意，付汝衣法，为第六代祖。火急速去，不得迟滞。思量即不中用，见性之人，言下须见。若如此者，轮刀上阵，亦得见之。

"Another day, the Patriarch summoned all his disciples and declared, 'Listen, to be freed from the cycle of birth-and-death is paramount. However, instead of spiritual liberation, most of you have been pursuing nothing but merits. How can merits free you if Intrinsic Nature is not realized? Now each of you, try to contemplate on the wisdom and Intrinsic Nature in you, and put the result of your contemplation in a poem and show me. If your poem corresponds with the Truth, I'll pass you the robe, the symbol of the Dharmic lineage, making you the Sixth Patriarch. Do as I said now! No delay! Deliberate conceptualization is of no use. One can realize Intrinsic Nature at any possible time, even in a battlefield with a sword in his hand.'

众得处分，退而递相谓曰：我等众人，不须澄心用意作偈，将呈和尚，有何所益？神秀上座，现为教授师，必是他得。我辈谩作偈颂，枉用心力。诸人闻语，总皆息心，咸言我等已后，依止秀师，何烦作偈？

"Having received these instructions, the disciples retreated and discussed, 'We don't have to make great efforts to compose the assigned poem, since Elder Shenxiu, our instructor, is bound to be the successor. Even if we try, our efforts would be in vain.' On hearing this, all decided likewise, 'We cannot compete with our instructor Shenxiu, the most promising candidate. Why bother trying?'

神秀思惟: 诸人不呈偈者,为我与他为教授师,我须作偈,将呈和尚。若不呈偈，和尚如何知我心中见解深浅？我呈偈意，求法即善，觅祖即恶,却同凡心,夺其圣位奚别？若不呈偈,终不得法。大难！大难！

"At this moment, Shenxiu thought, 'Others have given up out of respect to me as their instructor, so I must give it a try. If I don't, how can the Most Venerable evaluate my insight into Dharma? If I do, so long as I am after the Dharma, my intention will be wholesome; if I am after the title of Patriarch, my intention would be as unwholesome as someone pretending to be enlightened. But if I don't, I may miss the chance to hold the lineage. What a dilemma!'

五祖堂前，有步廊三间，拟请供奉卢珍画《楞伽经变相》及《五祖血脉图》，流传供养。

"In front of the hall of the Fifth Patriarch, there was a three-room sized corridor reserved for the *Illutrations of Laṅkāvatāra-sūtra* and the *Lineage of the Five Patriarchs* for future veneration by the painter Lu Zhen.

神秀作偈成已，数度欲呈，行至堂前，心中恍惚，遍身汗流，拟呈不得。前后经四日，一十三度呈偈不得。

"Upon completion of the task, Shenxiu went there several times, trying to submit his composed poem, but he failed. He was nervous and hesitant with sweat all over. He repeated this for four days with thirteen failed attempts.

秀乃思惟：不如向廊下书着，从他和尚看见，忽若道好，即出礼拜，云是秀作；若道不堪，枉向山中数年，受人礼拜，更修何道？是夜三更，不使人知，自执灯，书偈于南廊壁间，呈心所见。偈曰：
"Then a thought came to him, 'Maybe I can just write down the poem on the wall of the corridor since the Most Venerable will definitely see it when he passes by. If he approves it, I'll show up and humbly claim it. If, however, it fails to meet the standard, I have to admit that I have spent all these years in the mountain in vain, receiving undeserved respect. It would be pointless to continue my practice.' So, at midnight, a lamp in one hand, he secretly wrote down his insight on the wall of the South Corridor. The poem went:

身是菩提树，心如明镜台。
时时勤拂拭，勿使惹尘埃。
"My body is like a Bodhi-tree,
And my mind a dressing mirror,
Which needs to be constantly cleaned,
So that no dust accumulates.

秀书偈了，便却归房，人总不知。秀复思惟：五祖明日见偈欢喜，即我与法有缘；若言不堪，自是我迷，宿业障重，不合得法。圣意难测。房中思想，坐卧不安，直至五更。
"After finishing writing, he returned to his room. No one knew what he

did. Yet, he had another thought, 'If the Patriarch delights in the poem, it means I am on the right path of Dharma. If disapproved, I would know that I am still deluded and full of defilements, which disqualifies me from inheriting the title. I wonder what he will say.' He ached to know the result and this anxiety kept him restless till the daybreak.

祖已知神秀入门未得，不见自性。天明，祖唤卢供奉来，向南廊壁间绘画图相，忽见其偈。报言：供奉却不用画，劳尔远来。经云：凡所有相，皆是虚妄。但留此偈，与人诵持。依此偈修，免堕恶道；依此偈修，有大利益。令门人炷香礼敬，尽诵此偈，即得见性。门人诵偈，皆叹善哉。

"Meanwhile, the Patriarch already knew that Shenxiu didn't realize the Intrinsic Nature. At dawn, the Patriarch called the artist Lu to start the paintings only to find out that the wall had been occupied by a poem, so he apologized to the artist, 'It seems that no illustrations are needed for veneration any more. Really sorry for the trouble of coming all the way. As the sutra says, all phenomena are illusory. Instead of the paintings, let's keep the poem to facilitate everyone's practice. It can prevent its practitioners from getting reborn in the lower realms and bring them great benefits.' Then the disciples were told to pay tribute to the poem with burning incense and recite it devoutly so that they can realize Intrinsic Nature. They recited it as told and unanimously praised it.

祖三更唤秀入堂，问曰：偈是汝作否？

"At midnight, the Patriarch summoned Shenxiu to his room and asked,

'Is the poem written by you?'

秀言：实是秀作，不敢妄求祖位，望和尚慈悲，看弟子有少智慧否？
"Shenxiu answered, 'Yes, it was me who wrote it, but I didn't do it for the title. What I really wanted was your kind evaluation of my insights.'

祖曰：汝作此偈，未见本性，只到门外，未入门内。如此见解，觅无上菩提，了不可得。无上菩提，须得言下识自本心，见自本性，不生不灭。于一切时中，念念自见。万法无滞，一真一切真，万境自如如。如如之心，即是真实。若如是见，即是无上菩提之自性也。汝且去，一两日思惟，更作一偈，将来吾看。汝偈若入得门，付汝衣法。
"The Patriarch said, 'The poem shows that you haven't realized Intrinsic Nature: you are at the threshold, but haven't crossed it yet. It's impossible for you to attain the supreme enlightenment with such a view. To realize, here and now, your Intrinsic Nature, which neither arises nor ceases, is the way to obtain the supreme enlightenment. Intrinsic Nature manifests itself through moment-by-moment thoughts. All phenomena are connected without hindrance, so the reality in one exists in all. The Intrinsic Nature of all is what it truly is. And such state of mind is the reality. When so realized, one has truly realized the very Intrinsic Nature, which is called the supreme enlightenment. Now go back and compose a new one in a few days. If you get it right this time, I'll pass you the robe, the symbol of this lineage.'

神秀作礼而出，又经数日，作偈不成，心中恍惚，神思不安，犹如梦中，行坐不乐。

"After showing due courtesy, Shenxiu left. The next several days saw him still struggling to come up with a better poem. Hence, disturbed and distracted as if he were sleepwalking, he couldn't enjoy a single moment of his life.

复两日，有一童子于碓坊过，唱诵其偈。惠能一闻，便知此偈未见本性，虽未蒙教授，早识大意。遂问童子曰：诵者何偈?

"Two days later, a boy was reciting that poem when he passed by the rice mill. On hearing the poem, I could immediately tell that its writer had not realized Intrinsic Nature. On the other hand, I have a general idea of what Dharma is despite the fact that I have not received any teaching from the Master. Then I asked the boy what he was reciting.

童子曰：尔这獦獠不知，大师言：世人生死事大，欲得传付衣法，令门人作偈来看。若悟大意，即付衣法，为第六祖。神秀上座，于南廊壁上，书无相偈，大师令人皆诵，依此偈修，免堕恶道；依此偈修，有大利益。

"The boy replied, 'You barbarian don't know? The Master said what is paramount is to be freed from the cycle of birth-and-death, so he ordered each disciple to compose a poem on their insight into Intrinsic Nature and show it to him, if any poem reveals a significant insight, its author will receive the symbolic robe, which will make him the Sixth Patriarch. Elder Shenxiu has already written a Formless Poem on the wall of the South Corridor, and the Master ordered others to practice accordingly. In so doing, its reciters will avoid rebirth in the lower realms and gain significant benefits.'

惠能曰：我亦要诵此，结来生缘。上人！我此踏碓，八个余月，未曾行到堂前，望上人引至偈前礼拜。
"Then I said, 'I'd also like to recite that poem for a better rebirth. However, my good friend, I haven't even approached the Master's chamber since I started working in the mill eight months ago. Could you please take me there to pay tribute to the poem?'

童子引至偈前礼拜，惠能曰：惠能不识字，请上人为读。
"Then the boy led me to the poem, to which I bowed, and I said, 'I cannot read. Could any friend read it for me?'

时有江州别驾，姓张，名日用，便高声读。惠能闻已，遂言: 亦有一偈，望别驾为书。
"At that moment, a government official named Zhang Riyong from Jiangzhou happened to be there, so he read it aloud to me. After hearing it, I said to him, 'I also have a poem. Could you please write it down for me?'

别驾言：汝亦作偈，其事希有！
"The official was surprised, 'You write poems? Unbelievable!'

惠能向别驾言：欲学无上菩提，不得轻于初学。下下人有上上智，上上人有没意智。若轻人，即有无量无边罪。

"I retorted, 'A practitioner aimed at the supreme enlightenment shall never belittle a beginner. People low in social status may have supreme wisdom while those at the top of social hierarchy may sometimes lose their wisdom. Belittling others will result in immeasurable unwholesome karma.'

别驾言：汝但诵偈，吾为汝书。汝若得法，先须度吾，勿忘此言。

"The official responded, 'Alright, please share with me your poem and I'll write it down for you. Once you gain spiritual fruits, you have to deliver me first. This is our deal.'

惠能偈曰：

"The poem reads:

菩提本无树，明镜亦非台。
本来无一物，何处惹尘埃。

"The Bodhi-tree and the mirror
Are nothing but designations.
Ultimately, they do not exist,
Let alone a place to collect the dust.

书此偈已，徒众总惊，无不嗟讶，各相谓言：奇哉！不得以貌取人，何得多时使他肉身菩萨。

"The poem shocked everyone present and they all exclaimed, 'Amazing! We shall never judge a person by his appearance! Since when has he transformed into a living Bodhisattva?'

祖见众人惊怪，恐人损害，遂将鞋擦了偈，曰：亦未见性。众以为然。
"The Patriarch was afraid that such admiration for my poem might cause someone to harm me, so he rubbed it off with his shoe and commented, 'This poem shows no realization of Intrinsic Nature, either.' And the disciples agreed.

次日，祖潜至碓坊，见能腰石舂米，语曰：求道之人，为法忘躯，当如是乎？乃问曰：米熟也未？
"The next day, the Patriarch sneaked into the mill, where I worked. When he saw that I was husking the rice with a stone fastened to my waist, he remarked, 'A Dharma-seeker is supposed to dedicate himself to Dharma without much physical concerns, isn't he?' And he continued, 'Is the rice fully husked?'

惠能曰：米熟久矣，犹欠筛在。
"I replied, 'The husks have been removed already, but I still need to sift them out.'

祖以杖击碓三下而去。惠能即会祖意，三鼓入室。
"Then he struck the mortar three times with his staff and left. Immediately, I understood what he meant. Keeping his secret message in mind, I went to his chamber when the nightwatch hit the drum three times, tolling the time of the night.

祖以袈裟遮围，不令人见，为说《金刚经》。至"应无所住而生其心"，惠能言下大悟，一切万法，不离自性。

"He gave me a private lecture on *The Diamond Sutra* under the cover of his robe. Upon hearing the sentence of 'Use your mind responsively without any attachment', I suddenly had a thorough realization that nothing is apart from Intrinsic Nature.

遂启祖言：

"I summarize my realization as follows:

何期自性，本自清净；
何期自性，本不生灭；
何期自性，本自具足；
何期自性，本无动摇；
何期自性，能生万法。

"Intrinsic Nature is pure in itself all along;
Intrinsic Nature never arises nor ceases;
Intrinsic Nature is self-contained all along;
Intrinsic Nature never changes;
Intrinsic Nature manifests everything all along.

祖知悟本性，谓惠能曰：不识本心，学法无益。若识自本心，见自本性，即名丈夫、天人师、佛。

"Acknowledging my enlightenment, he said, 'If whatever you learned does not lead to Intrinsic Nature, such learning amounts to nothing. If you have realized Intrinsic Nature, you deserve the titles of Spiritual Mentor, Teacher of Deities and Humans, and Buddha.'

三更受法，人尽不知，便传顿教及衣钵。云：汝为第六代祖，善自护念，广度有情，流布将来，无令断绝。听吾偈曰：
"Then, unknown to others at midnight, I received the Teaching of Sudden Enlightenment along with the robe and the bowl. The Patriarch said, 'Now you are the Sixth Patriarch, so always stay mindful and dedicate yourself to the liberation of sentient beings and the spread of this teaching so that it will not disappear. Listen to this poem:

有情来下种，因地果还生。
无情亦无种，无性亦无生。
"In the fertile field of sentient beings' minds,
Dharma seeds shall be sown,
Where Buddha fruit
Will ripen eventually.
Whereas non-sentient beings,
Like barren fields,
Never possess the potential
To bear Buddha fruit.

祖复曰：昔达摩大师，初来此土，人未之信，故传此衣，以为信体，代代相承。法则以心传心，皆令自悟自解。自古，佛佛惟传本体，师师密付本心。衣为争端，止汝勿传。若传此衣，命如悬丝，汝须速去，恐人害汝。

“The Patriarch continued, ‘When Master Bodhidharma, [the First Patriarch,] arrived in China, nobody trusted him, so he showed Buddha’s robe to legitimize his lineage and ordered his disciples to pass it down. Dharma, however, can only be transmitted through one mind illuminating another, with the latter to be transformed on its own. Traditionally, the teaching of original mind was transmitted between Buddhas and masters in an esoteric manner. The robe is the cause of conflict, so the practice of passing it shall end with you. Otherwise, the life of its bearer will be endangered. Run! Run for your life! Lest people will harm you.’

惠能启曰：向甚处去?
“Then I asked, ‘Where am I supposed to go?’

祖云：逢怀则止，遇会则藏。
“The Patriarch replied, ‘Don’t go further once you reach Huai (Ji), and lay low in a place called (Si) Hui.’

惠能三更领得衣钵，云：能本是南中人，素不知此山路，如何出得江口？
“At that midnight, I received the robe the bowl and the asked, ‘I am not a local here. I may get lost on my way to the ferry.’

五祖言：汝不须忧，吾自送汝。
“The Fifth Patriarch replied, ‘Don’ t worry. I will take you there.’

祖相送直至九江驿，祖令上船，五祖把橹自摇。惠能言：请和尚坐，弟子合摇橹。祖云：合是吾渡汝。惠能云：迷时师度，悟了自度；度名虽一，用处不同。惠能生在边方，语音不正，蒙师传法，今已得悟，只合自性自度。祖云：如是！如是！以后佛法，由汝大行。汝去三年，吾方逝世。汝今好去，努力向南，不宜速说，佛法难起。

"The Patriarch took me all the way to the ferry of Jiujiang. He told me to get on the boat, and then he started to row the boat. I told him, 'Master, please take a seat. Let me do the rowing.' And he said, 'Let me be your ferryman.' I replied, 'If a disciple is deluded, he needs a ferryman to cross over to the other shore. Once the disciple is enlightened, he can be his own ferryman. Though used many times, 'ferryman' bears different meanings. I was born in an uncivilized place and hence considered vulgar. Regardless, you took me as your disciple and taught me Dharma. Now that I am enlightened, I shall cross over to the other shore by myself through Intrinsic Nature.'

The Patriarch praised, 'Right! Right! From now on, you shall shoulder the burden of popularizing the Dharma. I still have three more years to live after your departure. Now, have a good journey and try to get to the south. You'd better not start teaching Dharma too soon because it's difficult to be accepted [without conditions].'

惠能辞违祖已，发足南行。两月中间，至大庾岭。（五祖归，数日不上堂。众疑，诣问曰：和尚少病少恼否？曰：病即无。衣法已南矣。问：谁人传授？曰：能者得之。众乃知焉）逐后数百人来，欲夺衣钵。

"After bidding farewell to the Patriarch, I set off for the south. Two months later, I arrived at Dayu Mountain. (Since the Patriarch returned to the monastery, he had been absent from the services for several days. The disciples were concerned and asked, 'Most Venerable, have you been feeling sick or upset?' The Patriarch said, 'I am fine, but my robe and Dharma have been taken to the south.' Then they asked, 'Who took them?' The Patriarch answered in a pun, 'The capable one'. Hearing this, everyone came to realize who he was referring to.) Soon, hundreds of people started their hunting in attempt to take the robe and the bowl.

一僧俗姓陈，名惠明。先是四品将军，性行粗慥，极意参寻，为众人先，趁及惠能。惠能掷下衣钵于石上，云：此衣表信，可力争耶？能隐草莽中。惠明至，提掇不动，乃唤云：行者！行者！我为法来，不为衣来。

"One of the monks Huiming, previously a violent general surnamed Chen, was so anxious to catch me that he was the one who tracked me down. [Having sensed the danger], I placed the robe and the bowl on a rock and said, 'How could the robe be taken by force since it represents Dharma?' Then I hid myself in the grass. Huiming ran up to the robe and the bowl but failed to pick them up, so he called, 'Sir, Sir! I did not come for the robe; I came for Dharma.'

惠能遂出，坐盘石上。惠明作礼云：望行者为我说法。惠能云：汝既为法而来，可屏息诸缘，勿生一念，吾为汝说。明良久，惠能云：不思善，不思恶，正与么时，那个是明上座本来面目？惠明言下大悟。复问云：上来密语密意外，还更有密意否？
"Then I came out and sat on the rock in a lotus position. Huiming spoke to me with a gesture of courtesy, 'May I receive some teaching from you, Sir?' I said, 'If you truly come for Dharma, detach your mind from any distraction and thought. Then, I'll teach you.' After a while, I started, 'When neither the wholesome nor the unwholesome arise in your mind, who exactly are you at that moment?' On hearing this, Huiming gained a profound insight. And then he continued to ask, 'Besides these esoteric words what else can you teach me?'

惠能云：与汝说者，即非密也；汝若返照，密在汝边。明曰：惠明虽在黄梅，实未省自己面目。今蒙指示，如人饮水，冷暖自知。今行者即惠明师也。惠能曰：汝若如是，吾与汝同师黄梅，善自护持。明又问：惠明今后向甚处去？惠能曰：逢袁则止，遇蒙则居。明礼辞。（明回至岭下，谓趁众曰：向陟崔嵬，竟无踪迹，当别道寻之。趁众咸以为然。惠明后改道明，避师上字。）
"I said, 'Anything that can be verbally taught to you is no longer esoteric. Once you direct your attention inward, you will find the esoteric.' Huiming replied, 'I have been practicing in Huangmei [for a long time], but I have not realized who exactly I am. Thanks to your guidance, now I have. It's something that can only be experienced by oneself. This is like only by drinking it can you know whether the water is hot or cold. You are truly my Master.' I said, 'We are merely Dharma brothers under the same master in Huangmei. If you have truly realized who exactly you are, you can rely on yourself

then.' Huiming asked further, 'Then where shall I go now? ' I replied, 'Stop at Yuan and stay at Meng.' Then, Huiming thanked me and left. (When Huiming returned to the foot of the mountain, he told the other chasers, 'Just now I climbed up there and even searched the pathless places, but I found no trace of him. We'd better try somewhere else.' Everyone believed him. Since Huiming and Huineng shared the same character in their names, the former changed his name into Daoming out of his respect to Master Huineng.)

惠能后至曹溪，又被恶人寻逐，乃于四会避难猎人队中，凡经一十五载，时与猎人随宜说法。猎人常令守网，每见生命尽放之。每至饭时，以菜寄煮肉锅。或问，则对曰：但吃肉边菜。
"After I arrived in Caoxi, I was still chased by the vicious, so I hid myself in a group of hunters in Sihui for about 15 years. During that time, I would share Dharma with them whenever appropriate. The hunters asked me to keep an eye on the snares. I would always set the animals free whenever they were caught. For meals, I had to add vegetarian food alongside the meat in their pot. My behaviour made them curious, so I would stress, 'I am a vegetarian.'

一日思惟：时当弘法，不可终遁。遂出，至广州法性寺，值印宗法师讲《涅槃经》。时有风吹幡动，一僧曰风动，一僧曰幡动，议论不已。惠能进曰：不是风动，不是幡动，仁者心动。一众骇然。
"One day, it occurred to me that I could not keep hiding like this forever. It was time for me to start teaching. So I set off and later arrived at Faxing Temple in Guangzhou, where Venerable Yinzong

was teaching the *Mahāparinirvāṇa-sūtra* then. At that moment, a banner was wavering in the breeze. Over this, two monks started an argument on what exactly was moving. One maintained it was the breeze while the other insisted it was the banner. Then I weighed in, 'It was neither the breeze nor the banner. But it was your mind that moved.' Everyone was amazed by my words.

印宗延至上席，征诘奥义，见惠能言简理当，不由文字。宗云：行者定非常人，久闻黄梅衣法南来，莫是行者否？惠能曰：不敢。宗于是作礼。告请传来衣钵，出示大众。

"Even Venerable Yinzong invited me to take the seat of honor and asked me some challenging questions. Impressed by my concise and plain answers, he asked me, 'You must be somebody. I heard long time ago that the inheritor of the robe and Dharma of Huangmei had reached the south. Is it you?' I replied, 'Well, I'm unworthy of that title.' Then he greeted me politely and requested a display of the robe and the bowl.

宗复问曰：黄梅付嘱，如何指授？惠能曰：指授即无，惟论见性，不论禅定解脱。宗曰：何不论禅定解脱？能曰：为是二法，不是佛法，佛法是不二之法。宗又问：如何是佛法不二之法？惠能曰：法师讲《涅槃经》，明佛性是佛法不二之法。如高贵德王菩萨白佛言：犯四重禁，作五逆罪，及一阐提等，当断善根佛性否？佛言：善根有二，一者常，二者无常，佛性非常非无常，是故不断，名为不二。一者善，二者不善，佛性非善非不善，是名不二。蕴之与界，凡夫见二，智者了达，其性无二。无二之性，即是佛性。

"He then continued, 'What teaching did you receive from [the Fifth Patriarch in] Huangmei?' I answered, 'He taught me nothing but realization of Intrinsic Nature. Meditative concentration and liberation find no place in his teaching.' He asked in surprise, 'They don't? Why?' I explained, 'They fall into duality, which goes against Dharma. The real Dharma is of non-duality.' He went on, 'What do you mean by non-duality?' I replied, 'It is Buddha Nature according to *Mahāparinirvāṇa-sūtra*, the very scripture you are teaching. For example, in the sutra, Lofty-virtuous-king Bodhisattva asked Buddha, 'Is it true that some beings are deprived of Buddha Nature, such as ordained transgressors of Four Major Precepts, violators of the Five Extreme Violations, and Icchantika[①]?' The Buddha replied, 'There are two wholesome roots, one being permanent, and the other impermanent. Yet Buddha Nature is neither, and can not be deprived of, hence non-duality. Things can be wholesome or unwholesome, but Buddha Nature belongs to neither, hence non-duality. The unenlightened hold a dualistic view on Aggregates and Elements but the wise well understand their non-dualistic nature, which is exactly Buddha Nature.'

---

① Icchantika: A term used in the Mahayana tradition to refer to a class of beings who have lost all potential to achieve enlightenment or buddhahood. (Buswell Jr., R.E. & Lopez Jr., D.S. *The Princeton Dictionary of Buddhism*. Princeton: Princeton University Press, 2014, p.370.)

印宗闻说，欢喜合掌，言：某甲讲经，犹如瓦砾；仁者论义，犹如真金。于是为惠能剃发，愿事为师。

"Happy with what I said, Venerable Yinzong joined his palms and praised, 'My teaching is like debris while yours is like pure gold.' Then, he shaved my hair to make me a monk, [instead of his disciple] he treated me as his master.

惠能遂于菩提树下开东山法门。惠能于东山得法，辛苦受尽，命似悬丝。今日得与使君官僚、僧尼道俗同此一会，莫非累劫之缘，亦是过去生中供养诸佛，同种善根，方始得闻如上顿教得法之因。教是先圣所传，不是惠能自智。愿闻先圣教者，各令净心。闻了各自除疑，如先代圣人无别。一众闻法，欢喜作礼而退。

"Then under the Bodhi tree, I started to disseminate the teaching from East Mountain, Huangmei, 'East Mountain was the place where I received this teaching despite hardship and life-threatening danger. Today, the reason we are here to listen to this teaching of Sudden Enlightenment is because of merits we have accumulated for eons or because of the wholesome roots resulting from making offerings to buddhas in the past. This teaching was passed down from previous sages, not something invented by me. Those who are eager to hear the teaching, clear your mind first. If your doubts are cleared after hearing this, you will be on a par with previous sages.' The audience rejoiced over the Dharma talk and left after making a gesture of courtesy."

般若品第二
Chapter 2 On Prajñā

次日，韦使君请益。师升座，告大众曰：总净心念“摩诃般若波罗蜜多”。复云：善知识！菩提般若之智，世人本自有之；只缘心迷，不能自悟，须假大善知识，示导见性。当知愚人智人，佛性本无差别，只缘迷悟不同，所以有愚有智。吾今为说摩诃般若波罗蜜法，使汝等各得智慧。志心谛听！吾为汝说。

The next day, Prefect Wei requested the Master to teach more. The Master took his seat and addressed the assembly, “You shall clear your mind and recite ‘*mahāprajñāpāramitā*’”. He continued, “My Dharma friends, originally we have the awakening wisdom. However, our deluded mind can’t realize Intrinsic Nature on its own, so guidance from an advanced spiritual teacher is necessary. It must be noted that there is no difference in Buddha Nature between the deluded and the wise; the difference only lies in the realization of it. Today I am going to teach you *mahāprajñāpāramitā* so that you can obtain wisdom. Listen carefully! I’ll start now.

善知识！世人终日口念般若，不识自性般若，犹如说食不饱。口但说空，万劫不得见性，终无有益。

“My Dharma friends, people chant *prajñā* all the time without realizing it. This is like talking about food in an attempt to make the stomach full. Talking about emptiness amounts to nothing. Even though you keep chanting it for eons, Intrinsic Nature eludes you.

善知识！"摩诃般若波罗蜜"是梵语，此言"大智慧到彼岸"。此须心行，不在口念。口念心不行，如幻、如化、如露、如电；口念心行，则心口相应。本性是佛，离性无别佛。

"My Dharma friends, *mahāprajñāpāramitā* is Sanskrit. In our language, it means 'the great wisdom leading to the other shore'. The practice requires contemplation rather than mechanical repetition. Otherwise, the effect of your practice will be unstable like a mirage, a dewdrop or a flash of lightening. Chanted with contemplation, it will make the mind consistent with the speech. Intrinsic Nature itself is Buddha, and apart from it there is no Buddha to be found.

何名"摩诃"？"摩诃"是大。心量广大，犹如虚空，无有边畔，亦无方圆大小，亦非青黄赤白，亦无上下长短，亦无瞋无喜，无是无非，无善无恶，无有头尾。诸佛刹土，尽同虚空。世人妙性本空，无有一法可得，自性真空，亦复如是。

"What does '*mahā*' mean? It means 'great'. The awakened mind is all-encompassing and empty, like space. It can't be conceptualized in terms of shape, color, position, length, emotion, truth, morality, or sequence. So are the Buddha Lands. Likewise, originally everyone's nature is empty, within which nothing exists.

善知识！莫闻吾说空，便即着空。第一莫着空，若空心静坐，即着无记空。

"So my Dharma friends, you shall never attach to emptiness when you hear these words. Never! If you practice sitting with such attachment, you'll end up falling into a form of emptiness that is not conducive to liberation.

善知识！世界虚空，能含万物色像：日月星宿，山河大地，泉源溪涧，草木丛林，恶人善人，恶法善法，天堂地狱，一切大海，须弥诸山，总在空中。世人性空亦复如是。

"My Dharma friends, the space encompasses everything: celestial bodies, terrains, waters, plants, the wholesome, the unwholesome, heavens and hells, oceans and all mountains including Sumeru. So it is with the emptiness of our nature.

善知识！自性能含万法是大，万法在诸人性中。若见一切人恶之与善，尽皆不取不舍，亦不染着，心如虚空，名之为大，故曰摩诃。

"My Dharma friends, Intrinsic Nature is described as 'great' as it can encompass everything. That is to say everything is within one's nature.When faced with the wholesome or the unwholesome, the mind remains empty like the space with no grasping, rejection, or attachment. Such state is called *mahā*.

善知识！迷人口说，智者心行。又有迷人，空心静坐，百无所思，自称为大。此一辈人，不可与语，为邪见故。

"My Dharma friends, the deluded talk while the wise contemplate. Also, some of the deluded claim the thoughtless experience in their sitting as great. Because people of this kind hold such a false view, they are not suitable for my teaching.

善知识！心量广大，遍周法界，用即了了分明，应用便知一切。一切即一，一即一切，去来自由，心体无滞，即是般若。
"My Dharma friends, our mind is vast, omnipresent, and omniscient with clarity if applied. Since that one is all and all is one, the mind comes and goes freely without hindrance. This realization is *prajñā*.

善知识！一切般若智，皆从自性而生，不从外入，莫错用意！名为真性自用。一真一切真。心量大事，不行小道。口莫终日说空，心中不修此行，恰似凡人自称国王，终不可得，非吾弟子！
"My Dharma friends, this wisdom arises from Intrinsic Nature, not from outside. Don't get it the other way round. It is the function of the true nature: one is real, all are real. The mind should focus on the great cause rather than the lesser path. Like a commoner who claims himself as a king, those who talk about emptiness without any contemplation will attain nothing. They are not my disciples!

善知识！何名般若？般若者，唐言智慧也。一切处所，一切时中，念念不愚，常行智慧，即是般若行。一念愚即般若绝，一念智即般若生。世人愚迷，不见般若；口说般若，心中常愚。常自言我修般若，念念说空，不识真空。般若无形相，智慧心即是。若作如是解，即名般若智。

"My Dharma friends, what is *prajñā*[1]? *Prajñā* is 'wisdom' in our language. The practice of *prajñā* requires a non-deluded mind that discerns at every moment under all circumstances. *Prajñā* ceases once the mind is deluded and arises when discernment appears. Talking about *prajñā* without realizing it, the deluded remain deluded. Talking about emptiness and claiming themselves as practitioners of *prajñā*, they remain ignorant of the ultimate emptiness. *Prajñā* is formless; it is the discerning mind. Understood in this way, such discernment is described as *prajñā*.

何名波罗蜜？此是西国语，唐言到彼岸，解义离生灭。着境生灭起，如水有波浪，即名为此岸；离境无生灭，如水常通流，即名为彼岸，故号波罗蜜。

"What does *pāramitā* mean? This Sanskrit term can be translated as 'leading to the other shore', meaning 'transcending arising and cessation'. When we are attached to phenomena, arising and cessation occur like waves. It is called 'this shore'. When we are detached from phenomena, there is neither arising nor cessation, as when water keeps flowing. It is called 'the other shore' or *pāramitā*.

善知识！迷人口念，当念之时，有妄有非。念念若行，是名真性。悟此法者，是般若法；修此行者，是般若行；不修即凡；一念修行，自身等佛。

"My Dharma friends, when chanting, the deluded are not free

---

① *Prajñā:* Sometimes it is translated as"discernment".

from distracting and judging thoughts. Practice discernment all the time, then you can realize your true nature. This is the doctrine of *prajñā* when understood; it is the practice of *prajñā* when followed. Without practicing it, you remain ordinary. Even when you practice it for a single moment, you are being on a par with Buddha.

善知识！凡夫即佛，烦恼即菩提。前念迷即凡夫，后念悟即佛；前念着境即烦恼，后念离境即菩提。

"My Dharma friends, ordinary beings are themselves Buddhas, and defilements① themselves Bodhi. Once you are deluded, you are ordinary; once you are awakened, you are a buddha. Once you are attached to phenomena, defilements arise; when you are detached from them, Bodhi manifests itself.

善知识！摩诃般若波罗蜜，最尊最上最第一，无住无往亦无来，三世诸佛从中出。当用大智慧，打破五蕴烦恼尘劳。如此修行，定成佛道，变三毒为戒定慧。

"My Dharma friends, *mahāprajñāparāmitā* is the noblest, the supreme and the foremost. It does not stay, leave or come. It is from which buddhas of all times arise. With strong discernment, you shall see through Five Aggregates② and put an end to defilements. If you practice in this way, you will definitely attain Buddhahood and are able

---

① Defilements: Kleśa, also "afflictions".

② Five Aggregates: Matter, sensation, perception, mental formations, and consciousness.

to transform the Three Poisons[1] into discipline, concentration, and wisdom.

善知识！我此法门，从一般若生八万四千智慧。何以故？为世人有八万四千尘劳。若无尘劳，智慧常现，不离自性。悟此法者，即是无念、无忆、无着，不起诳妄，用自真如性，以智慧观照，于一切法不取不舍，即是见性成佛道。

"My Dharma friends, according to this teaching, this very *prajñā* can produce 84,000 kinds of wisdom. Why? Because people have 84,000 kinds of defilements. If they have no defilements, they will find that their wisdom is always there and they have never been separated from Intrinsic Nature. Those who understand this teaching are free from thoughts, memories, attachments and delusions. They can discern everything without grasping or rejection. They have realized Intrinsic Nature and Buddhahood.

善知识！若欲入甚深法界及般若三昧者，须修般若行，持诵《金刚般若经》，即得见性。

"My Dharma friends, if you want to go deep into the Dharma Realm and concentration of *prajñā*, you must practice the path of *prajñā* and recite the *Diamond Sutra* so that you can realize Intrinsic Nature.

当知此经功德，无量无边，经中分明赞叹，莫能具说。此法门是最上乘，为大智人说，为上根人说。小根小智人闻，心生不信。

---

① Three Poisons: Craving, aversion and delusion

"You should know that the merit of this sutra is immeasurable and boundless; it is clearly praised in the sutra that there are ineffably profound merits. As the supreme vehicle, this practice is revealed for those with great wisdom and superior faculty. On the contrary, those with inferior faculty will find no faith in this teaching.

何以故？譬如天龙下雨于阎浮提，城邑聚落，悉皆漂流，如漂枣叶。若雨大海，不增不减。若大乘人、若最上乘人，闻说《金刚经》，心开悟解，故知本性自有般若之智；自用智慧，常观照故，不假文字。譬如雨水，不从天有，元是龙能兴致，令一切众生、一切草木、有情无情，悉皆蒙润。百川众流，却入大海，合为一体。众生本性般若之智，亦复如是。

"Why? Because they are unable to withstand the supreme teaching in the same way that settlements on the earth can't stand the downpour brought by *naga-s*, which will scour them away as if they were grass leaves. If it rains over the ocean, however, every drop will be received. In the same way, if people of great or supreme vehicle hear the teaching of the *Diamond Sutra*, their innate wisdom will dawn on them. Such wisdom beyond language can be used to discern everything. The rain is brought by the *naga-s*, not fortuitously from heaven, in the same way that Dharma is taught by Buddha, [not something stumbled upon,] nourishing everything, be it sentient or non-sentient. Thanks to the rain, various rivers come into being, and in turn, converge to form the ocean. Similarly, the minds of all sentient beings fuse into Intrinsic Nature.

善知识！小根之人，闻此顿教，犹如草木。根性小者，若被大雨，悉皆自倒，不能增长。小根之人，亦复如是，元有般若之智，与大智人更无差别，因何闻法不自开悟？缘邪见障重，烦恼根深，犹如大云覆盖于日，不得风吹，日光不现。般若之智亦无大小，为一切众生自心迷悟不同。迷心外见，修行觅佛，未悟自性，即是小根。若开悟顿教，不执外修，但于自心常起正见，烦恼尘劳常不能染，即是见性。

"My Dharma friends, on hearing this teaching of Sudden Enlightenment, those with inferior faculty are like plants with shallow roots that collapse in a heavy rain and fail to grow. They have the same innate wisdom with the wise, so why doesn't this teaching dawn on them? It is because of the severe hindrance caused by their false views and deep-rooted defilements. It is like the clouded sun that will not be visible until the wind blows. Wisdom itself can not be measured. But different people have different levels of wisdom: little in the deluded and much in the awakened. Without realizing Intrinsic Nature, those with deluded minds seek externally for Buddhahood in their practice. They are of inferior faculty. If you understand the teaching of Sudden Enlightenment, you'll not cling to anything external. Instead, you will always have right views and stay free from defilements. This is the realization of Intrinsic Nature.

善知识！内外不住，去来自由，能除执心，通达无碍。能修此行，与《般若经》本无差别。

"Then, My Dharma friends, you will not dwell on anything internal or external, moving freely without any attachment or hindrance. If you follow this practice, you'll attain exactly what is taught in the *Prajñāpāramitā Sutra*.

善知识！一切修多罗及诸文字、大小二乘、十二部经，皆因人置，因智慧性，方能建立。若无世人，一切万法本自不有。故知万法本自人兴，一切经书因人说有。缘其人中，有愚有智，愚为小人，智为大人。愚者问于智人，智者为愚人说法。愚人忽然悟解心开，即与智人无别。

"My Dharma friends, all sutras and other texts in twelve divisions of scriptures of great and small vehicles were established for beings with different levels of spiritual maturity. If there were no beings in the world, none of the ten thousand teachings would have appeared in the first place. Therefore, we know that all teachings and scriptures emerge for the sake of beings. Among a group of people, some are deluded and some are wise. The deluded are of inferior faculty and the wise superior. If the deluded request the wise to share a teaching, which brings sudden enlightenment, they are no longer different from the wise.

善知识！不悟，即佛是众生；一念悟时，众生是佛。故知万法尽在自心，何不从自心中，顿见真如本性？《菩萨戒经》云：我本元自性清净。若识自心见性，皆成佛道。《净名经》云：即时豁然，还得本心。

"My Dharma friends, a buddha would be an ordinary being if he were not awakened; an ordinary being is a buddha the moment when he is awakened. So we come to know that everything is within our mind. Why not realize Intrinsic Nature in our mind right away? The *Brahmajala Sutra* says, 'My Intrinsic Nature is pure by essence.' Whoever understands his own mind and realizes his Intrinsic Nature can attain Buddhahood. The *Vimalakīrti Sutra* says, 'At that very moment, he came to know his Original Mind.'

善知识！我于忍和尚处，一闻言下便悟，顿见真如本性。是以将此教法流行，令学道者顿悟菩提，各自观心，自见本性。

"My Dharma friends, when I was listening to Dharma from Most Venerable Hongren, I suddenly realized Intrinsic Nature upon hearing certain words. Therefore, I am passing on this teaching that leads to sudden enlightenment. Its practitioners should observe their mind so that they can realize Intrinsic Nature.

若自不悟，须觅大善知识、解最上乘法者，直示正路。是善知识有大因缘，所谓化导，令得见性。一切善法，因善知识，能发起故。三世诸佛、十二部经，在人性中，本自具有。不能自悟，须求善知识，指示方见。

"If you cannot attain enlightenment on your own, you must find an advanced spiritual teacher who is versed in the doctrine of supreme vehicle and directly shows you the right path. With great conditions, such a teacher can guide you to realize Intrinsic Nature. Everything wholesome can be brought forth by him. All buddhas, buddhas-to-be and twelve divisions of scriptures are available in your innate nature. If you can't realize it by yourself, you have to seek guidance from a teacher.

若自悟者，不假外求。若一向执谓须他善知识方得解脱者，无有是处。何以故？自心内有知识自悟。若起邪迷，妄念颠倒，外善知识虽有教授，救不可得。若起真正般若观照，一刹那间，妄念俱灭。若识自性，一悟即至佛地。

“However, if you have realized it by yourself, you don’t have to seek externally. For those who need a teacher, they should not think that their liberation must solely rely on the teacher. Why? Because you have an inner teacher that can help you achieve self-enlightenment. However, instructions of the teacher won’t help you if false, deluded or perverted views arise in your mind. Once you start contemplating with *prajñā* properly, all your deluded thoughts will instantly cease. If you realize Intrinsic Nature, you’ll ascend to Buddhahood simultaneously.

善知识！智慧观照，内外明彻，识自本心。若识本心，即本解脱。若得解脱，即是般若三昧。般若三昧，即是无念。何名无念？若见一切法，心不染着，是为无念。用即遍一切处，亦不着一切处；但净本心，使六识出六门，于六尘中无染无杂，来去自由，通用无滞，即是般若三昧，自在解脱，名无念行。若百物不思，当令念绝，即是法缚，即名边见。

“My Dharma friends, with discernment, you’ll experience luminosity internally and externally, and eventually realize Original Mind. If you realize your Original Mind, you’ll find that you are liberated in the first place. This is the concentration of *prajñā*, namely Free Mind. What is Free Mind? If you cognize anything without being attached to it, this is Free Mind. It can be applied anywhere without any attachment. Purify your Original Mind and allow Six Consciousnesses① to cognize Six Objects② through Six Gates③ freely without being defiled or hindered. This is the concentration of *prajñā*, liberation without hindrance, and is called the practice of Free Mind. If you try to think of nothing by eliminating all thoughts, that means you are preconditioned by the quasi-Dharma, an Extreme View④.

善知识！悟无念法者，万法尽通；悟无念法者，见诸佛境界；悟无念法者，至佛地位。

"My Dharma friends, those who understand the teaching of Free Mind will know everything, cognize what buddhas cognize, and ascend to Buddhahood.

善知识！后代得吾法者，将此顿教法门，于同见同行，发愿受持，如事佛故，终身而不退者，定入圣位。然须传授，从上以来默传分付，不得匿其正法。若不同见同行，在别法中，不得传付。损彼前人，究竟无益。恐愚人不解，谤此法门，百劫千生，断佛种性。

"My Dharma friends, if those in generations to come hear and practice this method of Sudden Enlightenment, then make a lifetime

---

① Six Consciousnesses: Visual Consciousness, Auditory Consciousness, Olfactory Consciousness, Gustatory Consciousness, Tactile Consciousness, and Mental Consciousness.

② Six Objects: Form, Sound, Smell, Taste, Tangible Objects, and Mental Objects.

③ Six Gates: Eyes, Ears, Nose, Tongue, Body, and Mind.

④ Extreme Views refer to the two extreme views as eternalism and annihilationism.

commitment to sharing and upholding it in the way they would serve Buddha, they will definitely become sages. You shall never hide this teaching, but carry it on without relying on words as what Buddha and Master Bodhidharma did. Don't transmit it to followers of other views, practices or teachings. Otherwise it will do patriarchs a disservice and bring no benefit. I'm afraid these people may be too deluded to understand, thus defaming it. As a result, they are deprived of potential to attain Buddhahood for hundreds of eons and thousands of lifetimes.

善知识，吾有一无相颂，各须诵取。在家出家，但依此修。若不自修，惟记吾言，亦无有益。听吾颂曰：

"My Dharma friends, I have a Formless Poem for you, both the laity and the monastics, to recite and follow. Practice according to it. It'll be useless if you only try to memorize it. Now listen!

说通及心通，如日处虚空，
唯传见性法，出世破邪宗。
法即无顿渐，迷悟有迟疾，
只此见性门，愚人不可悉。
说即虽万般，合理还归一，
烦恼暗宅中，常须生慧日。
邪来烦恼至，正来烦恼除，
邪正俱不用，清净至无余。

"Someone who teaches Dharma skillfully with an unobstructed mind,
His wisdom shines like the sun in the sky.
I give this teaching on how to realize Intrinsic Nature

To dispel all false teachings in the world.
Dharma is not to be considered as sudden or gradual,
But awakening from delusion can be slow or quick.
This gate leading to Intrinsic Nature
Is beyond the comprehension of the deluded.
Despite a myriad of ways to be expounded,
The principle is ultimately one.
Just like a dark house needs to be illuminated by the sun,
Defilements shall be dispelled by wisdom.
Defilements arise upon false thoughts
And cease upon right ones.
When neither is attached to,
Purity reveals itself without remainder.

菩提本自性，起心即是妄，
净心在妄中，但正无三障。
世人若修道，一切尽不妨，
常自见己过，与道即相当。
色类自有道，各不相妨恼，
离道别觅道，终身不见道。
波波度一生，到头还自懊，
欲得见真道，行正即是道。

"Bodhi is originally Intrinsic Nature,
But it will be deluded by a thought that arises.
Though clouded by delusion, the mind can be freed

From Three Hindrances[①] once its purity is restored.
If anyone follows this practice,
Nothing will hinder him.
If you often contemplate your own faults,
You'll be in accord with the Path.
Each being has his own path to follow,
Which does not cross with others'.
If you abandon your path and seek for an alternative,
You will never realize the Path.
Spending your life in hustle and bustle
Will leave you with regret in the end.
To realize the real Path,
Practice properly.

自若无道心，暗行不见道，
若真修道人，不见世间过。
若见他人非，自非却是左，
他非我不非，我非自有过。
但自却非心，打除烦恼破，
憎爱不关心，长伸两脚卧。
欲拟化他人，自须有方便，
勿令彼有疑，即是自性现。

"Lacking a mind towards the Path,

① Three Hindrances: The affliction-hindrances, the karma-hindrances, and the retribution-hindrances.

You are like walking in the darkness.
In the eyes of a true practitioner,
There is no fault in the world.
When you judge others,
At this very moment you are wrong.
If you think others have faults and you don't,
You are already wrong.
Just get rid of any inclination to judge,
And all your defilements will be dispelled.
With a mind free of hatred and love,
You can be at ease.
If you want to teach others,
You need to have skillful means.
You should clear their doubts
So that their Intrinsic Nature can reveal itself.

佛法在世间，不离世间觉。
离世觅菩提，恰如求兔角。
正见名出世，邪见名世间，
邪正尽打却，菩提性宛然。
此颂是顿教，亦名大法船，
迷闻经累劫，悟则刹那间。

"Dharma is in the mundane realm
From which awakening is inseparable.
To seek Bodhi outside of the mundane realm
Is like pursuing horns of a hare [that never exist].

Perceived with right views, everything appears to be supramundane;
With false views, mundane.
Without conceptualizing the right and the false,
Your Bodhi nature will clearly reveal itself.
This poem is a teaching of Sudden Enlightenment,
Also called 'the Grand Ship of Dharma'.
Those who fail to get it will remain deluded for eons,
While those who can get it will attain enlightenment in a flash."

师复曰：今于大梵寺说此顿教，普愿法界众生，言下见性成佛。时韦使君与官僚道俗，闻师所说，无不省悟。一时作礼，皆叹：善哉！何期岭南有佛出世。

The Master continued, "I gave this teaching at Dafan Temple today in the hope that all sentient beings can realize Intrinsic Nature and attain Buddhahood at once." Prefect Wei, other officials, the monastics and the laity were all inspired by the Master's teaching. They thanked the Master and praised, "Excellent! We never expected someone like Buddha could emerge in our prefecture, Lingnan."

决疑品第三
Chapter 3
Resolving the Doubts

一日，韦刺史为师设大会斋。斋讫，刺史请师升座，同官僚士庶，肃容再拜，问曰：弟子闻和尚说法，实不可思议。今有少疑，愿大慈悲，特为解说。

One day, Prefect Wei arranged a public vegetarian feast for the Master. After the feast, he ushered the Master to the seat. Then, along with his government colleagues and commoners, he tidied his dressing, bowed to the Master and asked, "Most Venerable, I was so amazed by your teaching. However, there are still some points I don't understand. Could you kindly explain them?"

师曰：有疑即问，吾当为说。

The Master said, "Just ask whatever you don't understand. I'll explain it."

韦公曰：和尚所说，可不是达摩大师宗旨乎？

The Prefect asked, "Is the essence of your teaching the same with that of Master Bodhidharma?"

师曰：是。

The Master answered, “Yes, it is.”

公曰: 弟子闻达摩初化梁武帝,帝问云: 朕一生造寺度僧,布施设斋,有何功德? 达摩言，实无功德。弟子未达此理，愿和尚为说。

The Prefect continued, “I heard that when Bodhidharma was teaching the Emperor Wu of Liang, the emperor asked him, ‘I have committed my life to building monasteries, encouraging renunciation and making donations. How much merit have I accumulated?’ Bodhidharma answered, ‘None.’ I don’t understand why. So please tell me.”

师曰：实无功德，勿疑先圣之言。武帝心邪，不知正法。造寺度僧，布施设斋,名为求福。不可将福便为功德。功德在法身中,不在修福。

The Master said, “Indeed no merit. Don’t doubt the words of the sage. Holding a false view, the emperor didn’t know what Dharma really was. By building monasteries, encouraging renunciation and making donations, he was only pursuing mundane benefits. Merit cannot be mistaken for benefits. Merit is in the body of Dharma, not from beneficial deeds.”

师又曰：见性是功，平等是德。念念无滞，常见本性真实妙用，名为功德。内心谦下是功，外行于礼是德。自性建立万法是功，心体离念是德。不离自性是功，应用无染是德。若觅功德法身，但依此作，是真功德。若修功德之人，心即不轻，常行普敬。心常轻人，吾我不断，即自无功；自性虚妄不实，即自无德。为吾我自大，常轻一切故。

The Master carried on, "Merit is about realizing Intrinsic Nature or the sameness of all. It is about freeing the mind from hindrance at every moment to realize the accurate function of Intrinsic Nature. It is about keeping a humble mind and behaving properly. It is about how everything is established on Intrinsic Nature and how the mind is detached from thoughts. It is about staying with Intrinsic Nature and avoiding defilements in its application. Follow these and you will find the true merit in the body of Dharma. To accumulate merit, one should respect every being without a belittling mind because belittling mind sustains self-attachment, thus no merit. Deluded by his illusory ego, a person cannot accumulate merit. This is because he has a sense of superiority and always belittles others."

善知识，念念无间是功，心行平直是德。自修性是功，自修身是德。

"My Dharma friends, merit is about uninterrupted mindfulness with authenticity. It is about trying to realize Intrinsic Nature and cultivating self-discipline.

善知识，功德须自性内见，不是布施供养之所求也。是以福德与功德别。武帝不识真理，非我祖师有过。

"My Dharma friends, merit is to be cultivated through Intrinsic Nature, not to be sought via donation. This is the difference between mundane benefits and merit. The emperor didn't know this; the patriarch's comment on his deeds was reasonable."

刺史又问曰：弟子常见僧俗念阿弥陀佛，愿生西方。请和尚说，得生彼否？愿为破疑。

The Prefect asked another question, “I often see Buddhists, both lay and monastic, recite the name of Amitabha Buddha in the hope of getting reborn in the Western Pure Land. Most Venerable, would you reveal whether they can be reborn there or not? May you dispel my doubt.”

师言：使君善听，惠能与说。世尊在舍卫城中，说西方引化经文，分明去此不远。若论相说里数，有十万八千，即身中十恶八邪，便是说远。说远为其下根，说近为其上智。

The Master said, “Prefect, listen well. I will explain it to you. According to the sutra taught by Buddha in the city of Śrāvastī, the Western Pure Land is not far away from here. Although it is widely believed that the Western Pure Land is thousands of miles away, this long distance is actually perceived by people with Ten Unwholesome Karma-s① and Eight Incorrect Practices② only. It is far for those with inferior faculty but near for those with superior wisdom.

人有两种，法无两般。迷悟有殊，见有迟疾。迷人念佛，求生于彼；

---

① Ten Unwholesome Karma-s: (1) killing, (2) stealing, (3) debauchery, (4) lying, (5) frivolous talk, (6) insulting, (7) gossiping, (8) coveting, (9) getting angry, and (10) holding false views.

② Eight Incorrect Practices: Incorrect View, Incorrect Thought, Incorrect Speech, Incorrect Action, Incorrect Livelihood, Incorrect Effort, Incorrect Concentration, and Incorrect Mindfulness.

悟人自净其心。所以佛言：随其心净，即佛土净。

"There is only one Dharma, but there are two kinds of people: those who are slow to awaken and those who are quick. Those who are not yet awakened recite Amitabha's name for rebirth in the Pure Land while those who are already awakened just keep purifying their mind. As Buddha said, 'Once the mind is purified, the land of a buddha appears pure naturally.'

使君东方人，但心净即无罪；虽西方人，心不净亦有愆。东方人造罪，念佛求生西方；西方人造罪，念佛求生何国？

"Prefect, as a person in this Eastern Land, you'll be free from unwholesome karma if your mind is purified. For those in the Pure Land, they could also have faults if their mind were not pure. If the Easterners get reborn in the West by reciting Amitabha's name, then what land could the Westerners get reborn in after they had produced unwholesome karma?

凡愚不了自性，不识身中净土，愿东愿西。悟人在处一般。所以佛言：随所住处恒安乐。使君心地但无不善，西方去此不遥。若怀不善之心，念佛往生难到。今劝善知识，先除十恶，即行十万；后除八邪，乃过八千。念念见性，常行平直，到如弹指，便睹弥陀。

"The deluded know nothing about Intrinsic Nature or their pure land within, so they long for various pure lands elsewhere. Whereas for the wise, it makes no difference wherever they are. Therefore, Buddha said, 'They can find peace wherever they go.' Prefect, as long as your mind is free from the unwholesome, the Pure Land would not be distant. If you have an unwholesome mind, it will be difficult to be reborn there even you keep reciting Amitabha's name. Now I advise you, my Dharma friends, to eliminate Ten Unwholesome Karma-s first so that you can make huge progress in your practice. Next, eradicate the Eight Incorrect Practices so that you make another huge progress. If you are in touch with Intrinsic Nature and an authentic mind at each moment, it will only take a flash to arrive in the Pure Land and see Amitabha.

使君但行十善，何须更愿往生？不断十恶之心，何佛即来迎请？若悟无生顿法，见西方只在刹那。不悟，念佛求生，路遥如何得达？
"Prefect, as long as you practice Ten Wholesome Karma-s[①], why bother vowing to be reborn there? But if you do not rid your mind of Ten Unwholesome Karma-s, how can Amitabha take you to his land? If you understand the Sudden Teaching of Non-arising, you will see the West instantly. Otherwise, how can you overcome such a long distance by simply reciting Amitabha's name?

惠能与诸人移西方于刹那间，目前便见。各愿见否？众皆顶礼云：若此处见，何须更愿往生？愿和尚慈悲，便现西方，普令得见。
"I will show you the West in a flash so that you can see it for yourself. Would you like to see it?"The assembly bowed to Huineng and said,"If

---

① Ten Wholesome Karma-s: (1) no killing, (2) no stealing, (3) no debauchery, (4) no lying, (5) no frivolous talk, (6) no insulting, (7) no gossiping, (8) no coveting, (9) no anger, and (10) no false views.

we could see it here, why do we need to seek rebirth there? May Most Venerable show it to us."

师言：大众，世人自色身是城，眼耳鼻舌是门。外有五门，内有意门。心是地，性是王。王居心地上。性在王在，性去王无。性在身心存，性去身心坏。佛向性中作，莫向身外求。

The Master said, "Everyone, your physical body is like a city, and eyes, ears, nose, tongue [and tactile faculty] the gates. These are Five Gates outside, and there is another inside—the mind. The mind is the land, and Intrinsic Nature is the king who is dwelling in the land. When Intrinsic Nature is present, the king is there. When it is absent, so is the king. Intrinsic Nature sustains the body and the mind. Without it, the body and the mind start to decay. Seek Buddhahood within, not elsewhere.

自性迷即是众生，自性觉即是佛。慈悲即是观音。喜舍名为势至。能净即释迦。平直即弥陀。人我是须弥。邪心是海水。烦恼是波浪。毒害是恶龙。虚妄是鬼神。尘劳是鱼鳖。贪瞋是地狱。愚痴是畜生。

"Those who are ignorant of Intrinsic Nature are ordinary beings while those who are aware of it are buddhas. The very compassion in you is Avalokitêśvarā (the Bodhisattva of Compassion) and the joy and equanimity Mahāsthāmaprāpta (the Bodhisattva of Great Power). Your very purified mind is Śākyamuni Buddha and your authenticity Amitabha Buddha. Self-attachment is as massive as the Mount Sumeru; the misled mind is as turbulent as the ocean; defilements are as incessant as the waves; viciousness in you is an evil naga, falsehood a ghost, and defilements dangerous aquatics. Greed and hatred are the states of hells; delusion is the state of animals.

善知识，常行十善，天堂便至。除人我，须弥倒。去贪欲，海水竭。烦恼无，波浪灭。毒害除，鱼龙绝。自心地上觉性如来，放大光明。外照六门清净，能破六欲诸天。自性内照，三毒即除。地狱等罪，一时销灭，内外明彻，不异西方。不作此修，如何到彼？

"My Dharma friends, if you always accumulate the Ten Wholesome Karma-s, you are at the gateway to heaven. The Sumeru of self-attachment will fall; the ocean of greed will dry up; the wave of defilements will calm; the aquatics of viciousness will disappear. Then the awakened Buddha Nature in your mind will illuminate and purify the Six Gates and dispel even desires of sensual heavens. The illumination of Intrinsic Nature can instantly eliminate Three Poisons and hell-bound karma-s, so both the inner and outer worlds can shine as bright as the Western Pure Land. But if you do not practice in this way, how can you reach there?"

大众闻说，了然见性，悉皆礼拜，俱叹善哉！唱言：普愿法界众生，闻者一时悟解。

Upon hearing the teaching, the audience clearly understood what Intrinsic Nature was, so they thanked the Master and praised him aloud, "May all beings who have heard the teaching get enlightened at once."

师言：善知识，若欲修行，在家亦得，不由在寺。在家能行，如东方人心善；在寺不修，如西方人心恶。但心清净，即是自性西方。
The Master said, “My Dharma friends, it’s alright to practice as a layperson. You don’t have to join the monastic order. A layperson who practices properly is like an Easterner with a wholesome mind, while a monastic who doesn’t practice is like a Westerner with an unwholesome mind. As long as the mind is purified, the Pure Land within appears.”

韦公又问：在家如何修行，愿为教授。师言：吾与大众说无相颂。但依此修，常与吾同处无别。若不依此修，剃发出家，于道何益？颂曰：
Prefect Wei continued to ask, “Could you please explain how to practice as a layperson?” The Master replied, “I am going to give you a Formless Poem. If you follow the teaching in this poem, it will be like practicing by my side. If you don’t, you can gain no benefit from Dharma even you are ordained. The poem reads:

心平何劳持戒，行直何用修禅，
恩则孝养父母，义则上下相怜。
让则尊卑和睦，忍则众恶无喧，
若能钻木出火，淤泥定生红莲。

“A peaceful mind will not be bothered by precepts,
And will not require deliberate cultivation.
A grateful mind brings filial piety,
And bears love to seniors and juniors.
A tolerant mind creates harmony,

And settles quarrels.
If drilling woods can produce fire,
A lotus is bound to grow out of mud.

苦口的是良药，逆耳必是忠言，
改过必生智慧，护短心内非贤。
日用常行饶益，成道非由施钱，
菩提只向心觅，何劳向外求玄。
听说依此修行，西方只在目前。

"Good medicine tastes bitter,
And frank advice sounds harsh.
Wisdom comes from corrected mistakes,
While hiding them betrays your shortcomings within.
Always be helpful in daily life,
For donating money alone doesn't determine the attainment.
Bodhi should be only sought from within,
So don't bother seeking elsewhere.
If you hear this instruction and practice accordingly,
The Western Pure Land is right in front of you."

师复曰：善知识，总须依偈修行，见取自性，直成佛道。法不相待，众人且散，吾归曹溪。众若有疑，却来相问。时，刺史官僚，在会善男信女，各得开悟，信受奉行。

The Master continued, "My Dharma friends, you should practice according to this poem to realize Intrinsic Nature and attain Buddhahood. Dharma does not wait for anyone. The discourse is over now and I'll go back to Caoxi. If you have any question, please come and ask." Inspired by the teaching, the Prefect, other officials and the Buddhist followers vowed to put it into practice.

定慧品第四
Chapter 4
On Concentration and Wisdom

师示众云：善知识，我此法门，以定慧为本。大众勿迷，言定慧别。定慧一体，不是二。定是慧体，慧是定用。即慧之时定在慧，即定之时慧在定。若识此义，即是定慧等学。

The Master addressed his audience, “My Dharma friends, the tenet of my teaching is concentration and wisdom. Do not be deluded and wrongly claim that concentration and wisdom are different. In fact, they are essentially united. Concentration is the essence of wisdom, while wisdom is the function of concentration. When wisdom is present, concentration appears in the form of wisdom; when concentration is present, wisdom appears in the form of concentration. When this is understood, you’ll be practicing wisdom and concentration at the same time.

诸学道人，莫言先定发慧、先慧发定各别。作此见者，法有二相，口说善语，心中不善，空有定慧，定慧不等。若心口俱慧，内外一如，定慧即等。自悟修行，不在于诤。若诤先后，即同迷人。不断胜负，却增我法，不离四相。

"Practitioners, don't say that concentration precedes wisdom, or vice versa. Those with such a view on Dharma have an unwholesome mind no matter how good their speech may sound, and they merely talk about concentration and wisdom without unifying them. Only when both speech and mind are consistently aligned with wisdom can concentration and wisdom be unified. Self-practice is not about arguing. Whoever argues about the sequence of these two is no more than a deluded person. With such a desire for winning the argument, attachment to self, external objects, and the Four Conceptualizations① will be reinforced.

善知识，定慧犹如何等？犹如灯光。有灯即光，无灯即暗。灯是光之体，光是灯之用。名虽有二，体本同一。此定慧法，亦复如是。
"My Dharma friends, what are concentration and wisdom like? They are like a lamp and light. When there is a lamp, there is light. When the lamp is no longer there, it turns dark. The lamp is the essence of the light, while the light is the function of the lamp. They do not share the same name, but in terms of essence they are the same. So are concentration and wisdom."

师示众云：善知识，一行三昧者，于一切处行住坐卧，常行一直心是也。《净名经》云：直心是道场，直心是净土。莫心行谄曲，口但说直，口说一行三昧，不行直心。但行直心，于一切法，勿

---

① Four Conceptualizations: Conceptualizations of self, individual, sentient being, and living soul.

有执着。迷人着法相，执一行三昧，直言常坐不动，妄不起心，即是一行三昧。作此解者，即同无情，却是障道因缘。

The Master addressed the audience, “My Dharma friends, a practitioner of One-practice Samādhi should keep an authentic mind in any situation: walking, standing, sitting, or lying. As the *Vimalakīrti Sutra* says, ‘An authentic mind is the place for practice and pure lands’. Do not practice with an unauthentic mind. Don’t merely talk about authenticity and One-practice Samādhi without being authentic at all. Rather, practice with an authentic mind and cling to nothing. Attached to the teaching literally, the deluded claim that One-practice Samādhi is about sitting motionlessly and having a thoughtless mind. Such a claim makes the deluded no different from non-sentient beings and thus obstructs the Path.

善知识，道须通流，何以却滞？心不住法，道即通流。心若住法，名为自缚。若言常坐不动是，只如舍利弗宴坐林中，却被维摩诘诃。

“My Dharma friends, the Path should be unobstructed, but why is it blocked? When the mind is unattached to doctrines, the Path is unobstructed. Otherwise, it creates fetters for itself. If long motionless sitting is correct, how come Śāriputra, who sat in this way in the forest, was scolded by Vimalakīrti?

善知识，又有人教坐，看心观静，不动不起，从此置功。迷人不会，便执成颠。如此者众。如是相教，故知大错。

“My Dharma friends, some teachers emphasize motionless sitting and observation of inner stillness. This is a misinterpretation of Dharma due to their delusion and attachment. There are so many who teach in this way, and it is completely wrong."

师示众云：善知识，本来正教，无有顿渐，人性自有利钝。迷人渐修，悟人顿契。自识本心，自见本性，即无差别。所以立顿渐之假名。
The Master addressed the audience, "My Dharma friends, the correct teaching is not to be described as sudden or gradual, but it has to be taught so to suit different faculties of beings. Once Intrinsic Nature is realized, there will be no difference between the two kinds of practitioners. So 'sudden' and 'gradual' are merely designated terms.

善知识，我此法门，从上以来，先立无念为宗，无相为体，无住为本。无相者，于相而离相。无念者，于念而无念。无住者，人之本性。于世间善恶好丑，乃至冤之与亲，言语触刺欺争之时，并将为空，不思酬害。念念之中，不思前境。若前念今念后念，念念相续不断，名为系缚。于诸法上，念念不住，即无缚也。此是以无住为本。
"My Dharma friends, it has been our tradition to regard Free Mind as the principle, Formlessness as the essence, and Non-dwelling as the foundation. Formlessness means the mind is detached from a form when cognizing it. Free Mind means the mind that is free from proliferation of thoughts. Non-dwelling is the essential quality of our Intrinsic Nature. The mind does not react either positively or negatively to anything in the world, good or bad, hostile or friendly, and it nullifies words that are offensive, deceptive or contentious, for the mind never lingers on anything in the past. However, if the mind dwells on the past, present and future, there will be an incessant

stream of thoughts; this state is bondage. The mind that never dwells on anything is free from bondage; this is what 'Non-dwelling as the foundation' is about.

善知识，外离一切相，名为无相。能离于相，则法体清净。此是以无相为体。

"My Dharma friends, detachment from all external forms is called Formlessness. When the mind is detached from forms, everything is pure in essence; this is what 'Formlessness as the essence' is about.

善知识，于诸境上，心不染，曰无念。于自念上，常离诸境，不于境上生心。若只百物不思，念尽除却，一念绝即死，别处受生，是为大错。学道者思之。若不识法意，自错犹可，更误他人。自迷不见，又谤佛经。所以立无念为宗。善知识！云何立无念为宗？只缘口说见性，迷人于境上有念，念上便起邪见，一切尘劳妄想，从此而生。自性本无一法可得。若有所得，妄说祸福，即是尘劳邪见。故此法门立无念为宗。

"My Dharma friends, the mind that is not defiled when cognizing an object is called Free Mind. Such a mind is detached from any object, upon which no judging thoughts arise. It is a great mistake to refrain from thinking and to eliminate all thoughts because annihilation of thoughts leads to death and rebirth. Heed my words, Dharma learners! It is forgivable for someone to be ignorant of the doctrine, but it's unforgivable to mislead others by distorting the teachings in Buddhist scriptures. We set Free Mind as the principle. My Dharma friends, why? The deluded merely talk about Intrinsic Nature, but their mind is still not free from judging thoughts. These thoughts then give rise to false views, the cause of all defilements and illusions. Ultimately, nothing exists in Intrinsic Nature. If you claim that things exist and they are either good or bad, it means you have defilements and false views. That’s why we set Free Mind as the principle.

善知识，无者无何事？念者念何物？无者无二相，无诸尘劳之心。念者念真如本性。真如即是念之体，念即是真如之用。真如自性起念，非眼耳鼻舌能念。真如有性，所以起念。真如若无，眼耳色声，当时即坏。

“My Dharma friends, ‘Free’ of what? A ‘Mind’ for what? ‘Free’ of duality and defilements. A ‘Mind’ for Suchness, or Intrinsic Nature. Suchness is the essence of mind, and mind is the function of Suchness. Instead of eye, ear, nose or tongue faculties, it is Suchness that gives rise to sentience as Suchness is the essence. Without it, seeing and hearing would be impossible.

善知识，真如自性起念，六根虽有见闻觉知，不染万境，而真性常自在。故经云：能善分别诸法相，于第一义而不动。

“My Dharma friends, Suchness will remain undefiled and free when it gives rise to sentience through which Six Faculties cognize objects. Just as the scripture says, ‘[Buddha] can cognize everything with Intrinsic Nature undisturbed.’”

坐禅品第五
Chapter 5
On Sitting Meditation

师示众云：此门坐禅，元不着心，亦不着净，亦不是不动。若言着心，心元是妄。知心如幻，故无所着也。若言着净，人性本净。由妄念故，盖覆真如，但无妄想，性自清净。起心着净，却生净妄。妄无处所，着者是妄。净无形相，却立净相，言是工夫。作此见者，障自本性，却被净缚。

The Master addressed the audience, "This sitting meditation is never about fixating on mental activities or purity in a motionless posture. Mental activities are illusory like a mirage, so there is nothing to fixate on. Though pure in essence, one's nature is veiled by illusory thoughts. Once unveiled, purity can be restored. The very intention to fixate on purity gives rise to an illusion, something that does not exist unless there is fixation. Anyone who imposes a form on purity—which has no form in the first place—and considers it to be attainment of some kind will be bound by purity and has their Intrinsic Nature clouded.

善知识，若修不动者，但见一切人时，不见人之是非善恶过患，即是自性不动。善知识，迷人身虽不动，开口便说他人是非长短好恶，与道违背。若着心着净，即障道也。

"My Dharma friends, a desirable motionless state is about undisturbed Intrinsic Nature. In such a state, there is no judgement towards all people. Although some deluded practitioners can stay in a motionless posture, they will judge once they start to talk, which means their practice is against the Path. Attachment to mental activities or purity obstructs the Path."

师示众云：善知识，何名坐禅？此法门中，无障无碍，外于一切善恶境界，心念不起，名为坐。内见自性不动，名为禅。

The Master addressed the audience, "My Dharma friends, what is meditation about? According to this teaching, the mind remains unobstructed under all circumstances, be they good or bad; it produces no judging thoughts and discerns the undisturbed Intrinsic Nature within. This is what meditation is about.

善知识，何名禅定？外离相为禅，内不乱为定。外若着相，内心即乱；外若离相，心即不乱。本性自净自定，只为见境，思境即乱。若见诸境心不乱者，是真定也。

"My Dharma friends, what is concentration about? Concentration is about being detached from external objects and being undisturbed within. Detachment leads to an undisturbed mind while attachment leads to a disturbed one. Originally, the mind is pure and still; it only reflects objects [as they are] but can be disturbed by discriminating thoughts. Concentration, in its true sense, refers to the state when the mind is undisturbed by any object.

善知识,外离相即禅,内不乱即定。外禅内定,是为禅定。《菩萨戒经》云:我本元自性清净。善知识,于念念中,自见本性清净。自修自行,自成佛道。

"My Dharma friends, concentration is about being detached from external objects and undisturbed within. The *Brahmajala Sutra* says, 'Intrinsic Nature is pure in essence.' So, My Dharma friends, at each moment, discern this purity of Intrinsic Nature by yourself, practice by yourself, and attain Buddhahood by yourself."

忏悔品第六
Chapter 6
On Repentance

时，大师见广韶洎四方士庶，骈集山中听法，于是升座告众曰：来，诸善知识！此事须从自性中起。于一切时，念念自净其心，自修自行，见自己法身，见自心佛，自度自戒，始得不假到此。既从远来，一会于此，皆共有缘，今可各各胡跪，先为传自性五分法身香，次授无相忏悔。众胡跪。

Once, scholars and commoners from Guangzhou, Shaozhou and other neighboring places gathered for Dharma talks by the Master in the monastery. After taking the seat, the Master addressed the audience, "Listen up, my Dharma friends, practice begins with Intrinsic Nature. At each moment, purify your own mind, practice by yourself, see your own Dharma-body and Buddha within, liberate yourself and discipline yourself. Only in this way can your journey pay off. It is our karmic connection that brought us here together. Now kneel down for the Perfume of Five Dharmic Aggregates of Intrinsic Nature, and then the Formless Repentance." Everyone did so.

师曰：一戒香，即自心中，无非、无恶、无嫉妒、无贪瞋、无劫害，名戒香。

The Master said, “The first perfume is the Perfume of Discipline: the mind is free of wrongness, evilness, jealousy, craving, anger, and harm.

二定香，即睹诸善恶境相，自心不乱，名定香。

“The second is the Perfume of Concentration: the mind remains undisturbed by objects, wholesome or unwholesome.

三慧香，自心无碍，常以智慧观照自性，不造诸恶；虽修众善，心不执着，敬上念下，矜恤孤贫，名慧香。

“The third is the Perfume of Wisdom: free of unwholesome karma-s, the unobstructed mind discerns Intrinsic Nature with wisdom and remains detached from wholesome deeds such as respecting the seniors and taking care of the helpless and the poor.

四解脱香，即自心无所攀缘，不思善，不思恶，自在无碍，名解脱香。

“The fourth is the Perfume of Liberation: the mind is free of attachment to the wholesome and the unwholesome.

五解脱知见香，自心既无所攀缘善恶，不可沉空守寂，即须广学多闻，识自本心，达诸佛理，和光接物，无我无人，直至菩提，真性不易，名解脱知见香。

“The fifth is the Perfume of the Liberating View: although the mind is completely free of attachment, it should not abide in this state. The practitioner should continue to learn extensively until he realizes Intrinsic Nature. He can master doctrines and associate with beings congenially without discriminating between self and others. Eventually, he will attain full awakening that won't change.

善知识！此香各自内熏，莫向外觅。今与汝等授无相忏悔，灭三世罪，令得三业清净。

"My Dharma friends, don't seek these Perfumes externally as they emanate from within. Now, I will teach you the Formless Repentance to eliminate all your unwholesome karma-s so that your bodily, verbal and mental actions can be purified.

善知识，各随我语，一时道：弟子等，从前念、今念及后念，念念不被愚迷染；从前所有恶业愚迷等罪，悉皆忏悔，愿一时消灭，永不复起。

"My Dharma friends, repeat after me together, 'May our mind not be defiled by thoughts of delusion in the past, present, and future. We repent of all our past unwholesome karma-s such as delusion so that they can disappear altogether for good.

弟子等从前念、今念及后念，念念不被憍诳染；从前所有恶业憍诳等罪，悉皆忏悔，愿一时消灭，永不复起。

"'May our mind not be defiled by arrogance or deceit at each moment of the past, present, and future. We repent of all our past unwholesome karma-s such as arrogance and deceit so that they can disappear altogether for good.

弟子等从前念、今念及后念，念念不被嫉妒染；从前所有恶业嫉妒等罪，悉皆忏悔，愿一时消灭，永不复起。

"'May our mind not be defiled by jealousy at each moment of the past, present, and future. We repent of all our past unwholesome karma-s such as jealousy so that they can disappear altogether for good.'

善知识，以上是为无相忏悔。云何名忏？云何名悔？忏者，忏其前愆。从前所有恶业、愚迷、憍诳、嫉妒等罪，悉皆尽忏，永不复起，是名为忏。悔者，悔其后过。从今以后，所有恶业、愚迷、憍诳、嫉妒等罪，今已觉悟，悉皆永断，更不复作，是名为悔。故称忏悔。凡夫愚迷，只知忏其前愆，不知悔其后过。以不悔故，前愆不灭，后过又生；前愆既不灭，后过复又生，何名忏悔？

"My Dharma friends, so this is Formless Repentance. What is repentance about? It is about thoroughly repenting of past faults such as evil deeds, delusion, arrogance, deceit, and jealousy so that they will never appear again. It is also about repenting of all future faults such as evil deeds, delusion, arrogance, deceit, and jealousy, and vowing not to produce them again since the truth is clearly understood now. However, the deluded only know about repenting of past faults but are not watchful for their recurrence in future. If your faults are not repented of and eliminated, they will reappear in future. If the faults keep showing up, what kind of 'repentance' is that?

善知识，既忏悔已，与善知识发四弘誓愿。各须用心正听：自心众生无边誓愿度，自心烦恼无边誓愿断，自性法门无尽誓愿学，自性无上佛道誓愿成。善知识，大家岂不道众生无边誓愿度？恁么道，且不是惠能度。

"My Dharma friends, now that you have repented, I will teach you how to make the Four Great Vows. Everyone, please listen carefully. I vow to liberate the innumerable sentient beings in my mind. I vow to eradicate the endless defilements in my mind. I vow to learn the infinite practicing methods within Intrinsic Nature. I vow to attain the supreme Buddhahood within Intrinsic Nature. My Dharma friends, we normally say that 'I' vow to liberate the innumerable sentient beings, don't we? But here, 'I' does not refer to a particular liberator, like Huineng.

善知识，心中众生，所谓邪迷心、诳妄心、不善心、嫉妒心、恶毒心，如是等心，尽是众生。各须自性自度，是名真度。

"My Dharma friends, 'sentient beings in the mind' refers to the wrong and deluded mind, the deceptive mind, the unwholesome mind, the jealous mind, the vicious mind, and other such minds. These are all 'sentient beings'. Each of them must be liberated within one's own Intrinsic Nature; this is called true liberation.

何名自性自度？即自心中邪见烦恼愚痴众生，将正见度。既有正见，使般若智打破愚痴迷妄众生，各各自度。邪来正度，迷来悟度，愚来智度，恶来善度。如是度者，名为真度。

"What is liberation within Intrinsic Nature? It is to liberate the sentient beings in the mind, namely the wrong views, defilements, and ignorance, through right views. Right views and wisdom can destroy such 'sentient beings' as ignorance and delusion so that all of them can be 'liberated'. Right views correct false ones; awakening dispels delusion; wisdom illuminates ignorance; the wholesome replace the unwholesome. Liberation in this way is true liberation.

又，烦恼无边誓愿断。将自性般若智，除却虚妄思想心是也。又，法门无尽誓愿学，须自见性，常行正法，是名真学。又，无上佛道誓愿成，既常能下心，行于真正，离迷离觉，常生般若，除真除妄，即见佛性，即言下佛道成。常念修行是愿力法。

"'I vow to eradicate the endless defilements'. It involves removing the illusory and judging mind by the wisdom of Intrinsic Nature. Next, 'I vow to learn the infinite practicing methods'. Learning, in its true sense, is when you can realize Intrinsic Nature and practice according to the authentic Dharma. Next, 'I vow to attain the supreme Buddhahood'. If you are committed to the authentic Dharma in your practice—which involves detaching yourself from delusion and [conceptualized] enlightenment, truth and falsehood through constant discernment—you will see Buddha Nature and attain Buddhahood at once. Always keep in mind these Four Great Vows as a part of your practice.

善知识！今发四弘愿了，更与善知识授无相三归依戒。善知识！归依觉，两足尊；归依正，离欲尊；归依净，众中尊。

"My Dharma friends, now that you have made the Four Great Vows, you can receive the Formless Precepts of the Three Refuges from me. My Dharma friends, take refuge in awakening, which can fully endow you with merit and wisdom; take refuge in the authentic Dharma, which can completely free you from desires; take refuge in purity, which can make you the most respected.

从今日去，称觉为师，更不归依邪魔外道。以自性三宝常自证明。劝善知识，归依自性三宝。佛者，觉也。法者，正也。僧者，净也。自心归依觉，邪迷不生，少欲知足，能离财色，名两足尊。自心归依正，念念无邪见，以无邪见故，即无人我贡高贪爱执着，名离欲尊。自心归依净，一切尘劳爱欲境界，自性皆不染着，名众中尊。

"From now on, take awakening as your teacher and never lend an ear to the evil or the heretical. Your own mind is always the witness of your refuge in the Triple Gem of Intrinsic Nature. I advise you, my Dharma friends, to take refuge in the Triple Gem of Intrinsic Nature. Buddha means awakening, Dharma authenticity, and Sangha purity. Taking refuge in awakening, your mind has no room for wrong views and delusion. With little desire, you are content and detached from greed and lust, hence 'fully endow you with merit and wisdom'. When your mind takes refuge in the authentic Dharma, it will be free of wrong views, discrimination between self and others, arrogance, craving and attachment, hence 'completely free you from desires'. When your mind takes refuge in purity, Intrinsic Nature is not affected by defilements, lust, craving, or even objects, hence 'make you the most respected'.

若修此行，是自归依。凡夫不会，从日至夜，受三归戒。若言归依佛，佛在何处？若不见佛，凭何所归，言却成妄。善知识，各自观察，莫错用心。经文分明言自归依佛，不言归依他佛。自佛不归，无所依处。今既自悟，各须归依自心三宝。内调心性，外敬他人，是自归依也。

“Following these instructions involves taking refuge in yourself. Ignorant of this, people only take the precepts of the Three Refuges in a ritualistic way day and night. You claim that you have taken refuge in a buddha, then tell me where he is. If you fail to do so, how can you say you have taken refuge in him? Your words make no sense. My Dharma friends, watch your mind and don't misdirect it. According to the scriptures, you shall take refuge in the buddha within instead of a buddha elsewhere. Otherwise, you will find no place to take refuge in. Now that you understand, please take refuge in the Triple Gem in your mind, which requires you to tame your mind and show respect to others. This is what I mean by 'taking refuge in yourself'.

善知识，既归依自三宝竟，各各志心，吾与说一体三身自性佛，令汝等见三身，了然自悟自性。总随我道：于自色身归依清净法身佛；于自色身归依圆满报身佛；于自色身归依千百亿化身佛。

“My Dharma friends, after taking refuge, now please pay attention to my teaching on the Three-body Buddha of Intrinsic Nature, so you may see the Three Bodies of Buddha, or Three Bodies, and realize Intrinsic Nature. Everyone, repeat after me: 'I take refuge in the Buddha of pure Dharma-body (dharmakāya) within my physical body; I take refuge in the Buddha of perfect Enjoyment-body (sambhogakāya) within my physical body; I take refuge in the Buddha of infinite Manifestation-body (nirmāṇakāya) within my physical body.'

善知识，色身是舍宅，不可言归。向者三身佛，在自性中，世人总有。为自心迷，不见内性，外觅三身如来，不见自身中有三身佛。汝等听说，令汝等于自身中，见自性有三身佛。此三身佛，从自性生，不从外得。

"My Dharma friends, you can't say the physical body is where you take refuge for it's just a temporary shelter. The so-called Three Bodies are within Intrinsic Nature and available to us all the time. However, due to your deluded mind, you fail to see Intrinsic Nature. As you search for Three Bodies elsewhere, you fail to look within. Please listen to my following teaching so that you can see Three Bodies within Intrinsic Nature. These Three Bodies can be found in Intrinsic Nature, not elsewhere.

何名清净法身佛？世人性本清净，万法从自性生。思量一切恶事，即生恶行。思量一切善事，即生善行。如是诸法，在自性中，如天常清，日月常明，为浮云盖覆，上明下暗。忽遇风吹云散，上下俱明，万象皆现。世人性常浮游，如彼天云。

"How to understand the Buddha of pure Dharma-body? Our pure Intrinsic Nature is where everything comes to be: unwholesome thoughts give rise to unwholesome deeds while wholesome thoughts to wholesome deeds. All things, within Intrinsic Nature, are as clear as the sky and as bright as the sun and the moon, but they will be veiled by thoughts in a way that the light is blocked by the cloud; when a wind dispels the cloud, everything will be clearly visible again. The cloud here is analogous to our capricious thoughts.

善知识，智如日，慧如月。智慧常明，于外着境，被妄念浮云盖覆自性，不得明朗。若遇善知识，闻真正法，自除迷妄，内外明彻，于自性中万法皆现。见性之人，亦复如是。此名清净法身佛。

"My Dharma friends, just like the sun and the moon, the discernment [of Intrinsic Nature] shines always. However, its radiance is blocked when Intrinsic Nature is clouded due to attachment to external objects and illusory thoughts. With authentic teachings from a spiritual master, delusion can be dispelled and everything, inside or outside, can be understood completely. This is the way Intrinsic Nature manifests itself. This is the case with those who have realized Intrinsic Nature. Only in this way should the Buddha of pure Dharma-body be understood.

善知识，自心归依自性，是归依真佛。自归依者，除却自性中不善心、嫉妒心、谄曲心、吾我心、诳妄心、轻人心、慢他心、邪见心、贡高心，及一切时中不善之行。常自见己过，不说他人好恶，是自归依。常须下心，普行恭敬，即是见性通达，更无滞碍，是自归依。

"My Dharma friends, you are taking refuge in the real Buddha only when your mind is taking refuge in Intrinsic Nature. Taking refuge in Intrinsic Nature is about eradicating jealousy, crookedness, selfishness, deception, scornfulness, arrogance, false views, boastfulness, and all unwholesome deeds. It is about always reflecting on your own faults rather than judging others. It is about being humble and respectful, which is a state of acceptance and non-resistance when Intrinsic Nature is realized.

何名圆满报身？譬如一灯能除千年暗，一智能灭万年愚。莫思向前，已过不可得。常思于后，念念圆明，自见本性。善恶虽殊，本性无二。无二之性，名为实性。于实性中，不染善恶，此名圆满报身佛。自性起一念恶，灭万劫善因；自性起一念善，得恒沙恶尽。直至无上菩提，念念自见，不失本念，名为报身。

"How to understand the perfect Enjoyment-body? In the way that a lamp can dispel long-lasting darkness, a flash of wisdom can eliminate deeply-rooted delusion. Do not let your mind dwell on what has passed, for it is no longer available. Focus on the present and the future; make sure that your mind is flawless and clear so that you can realize your original nature. The wholesome and the unwholesome may seem to be different, but they share the same nature, which is the true nature. Within this true nature, there is no attachment to either the wholesome or the unwholesome. This is how the Buddha of the perfect Enjoyment-body is understood. An unwholesome thought from Intrinsic Nature will nullify wholesome conditions accumulated for eons. Likewise, a wholesome thought can nullify unwholesome conditions that are as many as sand grains in the Ganges. See Intrinsic Nature in each moment without losing the original mind until you attain the supreme enlightenment. This is how the Enjoyment-body is understood.

何名千百亿化身？若不思万法，性本如空。一念思量，名为变化。思量恶事，化为地狱。思量善事，化为天堂。毒害化为龙蛇。慈悲化为菩萨。智慧化为上界。愚痴化为下方。自性变化甚多，迷人不能省觉，念念起恶，常行恶道。回一念善，智慧即生。此名自性化身佛。

“How to understand the infinite forms of Manifestation-body? If you don’t conceptualize anything, you will see your nature as it is—emptiness. Conceptualization even for a single moment brings about manifestations. Anything unwholesome leads to manifestation of hells, and anything wholesome leads to heavens; cruelty leads to *naga-s*; compassion, bodhisattvas; wisdom leads to higher realms; ignorance, lower realms. Unaware of Intrinsic Nature in its various forms, the deluded have a series of unwholesome thoughts that lead to unwholesome paths. The very instant you switch to a wholesome thought, wisdom arises. This is how the Buddha of Manifestation-body in Intrinsic Nature is understood.

善知识，法身本具，念念自性自见，即是报身佛。从报身思量，即是化身佛。自悟自修，自性功德，是真归依。皮肉是色身，色身是宅舍，不言归依也。但悟自性三身，即识自性佛。吾有一无相颂，若能诵持，言下令汝积劫迷罪，一时消灭。颂曰：

“My Dharma friends, when the original Dharma-body, or Intrinsic Nature, is discerned in each moment, there is Enjoyment-body. Once the Buddha of Enjoyment-body starts to discriminate, there is the Buddha of Manifestation-body. If you understand the merit of Intrinsic Nature and cultivate it, you are taking refuge in its true sense. This physical body, however, should not be taken as a refuge because it is nothing but a temporary shelter. Once you understand the Three Bodies of Intrinsic Nature, you realize the Buddha of Intrinsic Nature. I have a Formless Poem for you. Once internalized, it can instantly eliminate faults and delusion you have accumulated for eons. The poem reads:

迷人修福不修道，只言修福便是道，
布施供养福无边，心中三恶元来造。
拟将修福欲灭罪，后世得福罪还在，
但向心中除罪缘，各自性中真忏悔。
忽悟大乘真忏悔，除邪行正即无罪，
学道常于自性观，即与诸佛同一类。

"The deluded work for benefits instead of liberation,
Without knowing their difference.
Although they can gain immeasurable benefits through donation,
They still have defilements that originate from their mind.
Their efforts to eliminate these defilements by accumulating benefits
Will not fully pay off: benefits will be gained,
Yet defilements still remain.
It is only possible to uproot defilements
By resorting to Intrinsic Nature and repenting sincerely.
By following the way of repentance in the Great Vehicle,
They dispel delusion and follow the truth, thus no defilements.
If they discern everything within Intrinsic Nature,
They will be on par with buddhas.

吾祖惟传此顿法，普愿见性同一体，
若欲当来觅法身，离诸法相心中洗。
努力自见莫悠悠，后念忽绝一世休，
若悟大乘得见性，虔恭合掌至心求。

"Our patriarchs handed down this Sudden Teaching,
Hoping that all would realize what buddhas have realized: Intrinsic Nature.
If you want to pursue Dharma-body,
Purify your mind and detach yourself from all forms.
You should strive to realize Intrinsic Nature
Because this life can end at any time.
If you have a taste of Intrinsic Nature
Through the teaching of the Great Vehicle,
You should seek for it sincerely and wholeheartedly."

师言：善知识，总须诵取，依此修行。言下见性，虽去吾千里，如常在吾边。于此言下不悟，即对面千里，何勤远来？珍重，好去。一众闻法，靡不开悟，欢喜奉行。

The Master said, "My Dharma friends, recite this poem and practice accordingly. If you can realize Intrinsic Nature upon hearing my words, it's like I am always with you. Otherwise, your long journey here will not pay off even if we sit face to face. That's it. Wish you good luck!" Upon hearing this Dharma talk, the audience understood and were happy to put the teaching into practice.

机缘品第七
Chapter 7
On Opportunity and Condition

师自黄梅得法，回至韶州曹侯村，人无知者。时有儒士刘志略，礼遇甚厚。志略有姑为尼，名无尽藏，常诵《大涅槃经》。师暂听，即知妙义，遂为解说。尼乃执卷问字。

Having obtained the teaching from the Fifth Patriarch, the Master came back to Caohou (a village in Shaozhou) where he was unknown to people but well-treated by Liu Zhilue, a Confucian. Zhilue's aunt, a nun called Wujinzang, often chanted the *Mahāparinirvāṇa Sutra*. One time, the Master heard her chanting the sutra and immediately understood its profound meaning. He was willing to expound the sutra, so the nun presented the text.

师曰：字即不识，义即请问。

The Master said, "I can't read, but I can explain doctrines."

尼曰：字尚不识，焉能会义？

The nun was surprised, "How is it possible?"

师曰：诸佛妙理，非关文字。

The Master told her, “Doctrines have little to do with texts.”

尼惊异之，遍告里中耆德云：此是有道之士，宜请供养。有魏武侯玄孙曹叔良及居民，竞来瞻礼。时宝林古寺，自隋末兵火已废。遂于故基，重建梵宇，延师居之，俄成宝坊。

The nun was impressed by his answer and told all the elders in the village, “You should provide this master with material support for he is accomplished in Dharma.” Cao Shuliang, a descendant of Marquess Wu of the Wei dynasty, along with other residents hurried to pay homage. At that time, Baolin Temple—an old temple destroyed in a war at the end of the Sui dynasty—was rebuilt on its original site to house the Master. It soon became famous.

师住九月余日，又为恶党寻逐。师乃遁于前山，被其纵火焚草木，师隐身挨入石中得免。石今有师趺坐膝痕及衣布之纹，因名避难石。师忆五祖怀会止藏之嘱，遂行隐于二邑焉。

However, about nine months later, the villains started to hunt the Master down again. The Master went into hiding in a mountain, so the villains set fire to smoke him out. Thanks to the rocks that sheltered him from being burnt, the Master remained unharmed. Today, on one of these rocks, one can still find traces left by the Master while he was taking refuge there in lotus position; hence the name “Refuge Rock”. Later, the Master remembered his teacher’s instruction “Stop at Huai Ji and hide in Si Hui”, so he followed it.

僧法海，韶州曲江人也。初参祖师。问曰：即心即佛，愿垂指谕。
Once, Venerable Fahai from Qujiang, Shaozhou came to the Master for instruction, "May you explain the meaning of 'the mind is Buddha'."

师曰：前念不生即心，后念不灭即佛。成一切相即心，离一切相即佛。吾若具说，穷劫不尽。听吾偈曰：
The Master replied, "The mind refers to the state in which the previous thought doesn't arise, and Buddha refers to the state in which the next thought doesn't cease. The mind gives rise to all forms, and Buddha [Nature] is detached from these forms. This is something too much to elaborate on, so let me summarize it in this poem:

即心名慧，即佛乃定。
定慧等持，意中清净。
悟此法门，由汝习性。
用本无生，双修是正。

"Such a mind is wisdom, and here Buddha is concentration.
Practice wisdom and concentration at the same time,
So that the mind will be purified.
Whether you can understand this method of practice
Depends on your faculty.
As functions [of Intrinsic Nature],
Concentration and wisdom are empty.
[Though empty,] they are still necessary."

法海言下大悟，以偈赞曰：

Upon hearing these words, Fahai gained a profound insight and praised [the teaching] with another poem:

即心元是佛，不悟而自屈。
我知定慧因，双修离诸物。

"The mind is originally Buddha [Nature].
Ignorant of this, I thought I was inferior to buddhas.
Now, since I have understood the true meaning of
Concentration and wisdom,
I shall practice both to free myself from all forms."

僧法达，洪州人。七岁出家，常诵《法华经》。来礼祖师，头不至地。

Venerable Fada, who came from Hongzhou and joined the monastery at the age of seven, often chanted the Lotus Sutra. One day, he came to visit the Master. But when he was bowing down to the Master, his head was not pressed against the ground.

师诃曰：礼不投地，何如不礼？汝心中必有一物，蕴习何事耶？

The Master scolded him, "Better no homage than an insincere one! There must be something in your mind [that makes you so proud]. What have you been practicing?"

曰：念《法华经》已及三千部。

Fada replied, "I have already chanted the *Lotus Sutra* three thousand times."

师曰：汝若念至万部，得其经意，不以为胜，则与吾偕行。汝今负此事业，都不知过。听吾偈曰：

The Master said, “You can be my peer if you do not consider yourself to be superior after having chanted the sutra as many as ten thousand times and fully understood it. It’s a shame if you think your chanting is something. Now listen to my poem:

礼本折慢幢，头奚不至地？
有我罪即生，亡功福无比。

“Bowing is a practice to reduce arrogance.
Why are you reluctant to press your head against the ground?
The sense of superiority produces faults,
And eliminating it generates merits.”

师又曰：汝名什么？

The Master asked, “What is your name?”

曰：法达。

“Fada.”

师曰：汝名法达，何曾达法？复说偈曰：

The Master said, “Your name means ‘Dharma expert’, but are you really an expert in Dharma? I’ll give you another poem.

汝今名法达，勤诵未休歇。
空诵但循声，明心号菩萨。
汝今有缘故，吾今为汝说。
但信佛无言，莲花从口发。

"Although your name is 'Dharma expert'
And you do chant the sutra diligently and unceasingly,
Your chant is in vain.
Only when you know the mind can you be called a bodhisattva,
[an expert in Dharma].
I taught you this since we are karmically connected.
Only when you truly understand the wordless teaching of Buddha;
Can your chanting make the lotus bloom."

达闻偈，悔谢曰：而今而后，当谦恭一切。弟子诵《法华经》，未解经义，心常有疑。和尚智慧广大，愿略说经中义理。

After hearing the poem, Fada apologized for his ignorance, "From now on, I shall be humble. I have been chanting the *Lotus Sutra*, but I don't understand its meaning. I wish you could explain it to me because you are so wise."

师曰：法达！法即甚达，汝心不达。经本无疑，汝心自疑。汝念此经，以何为宗？

The Master said, "Fada, Dharma is always accessible, but your mind makes it out of reach. The sutra is clear beyond doubt, but your mind makes it dubious. Since you have chanted the sutra a lot of times, you must know its theme."

达曰：学人根性暗钝，从来但依文诵念，岂知宗趣？
Fada replied, “As a slow learner, I just literally chant it. How could I know its theme?”

师曰：吾不识文字，汝试取经诵一遍，吾当为汝解说。
The Master said, “I can’t read. Just chant it through and I’ll explain it to you.”

法达即高声念经，至《譬喻品》，师曰：止！此经元来以因缘出世为宗，纵说多种譬喻，亦无越于此。何者因缘？经云：诸佛世尊，唯以一大事因缘故，出现于世。一大事者，佛之知见也。
Fada then read the sutra aloud until the Chapter of Parables when the Master interrupted, “Stop there! This sutra explains the reason why buddhas appear in the world. Although there are many parables in the sutra, none of them goes beyond the theme. What is the reason then? The sutra says, ‘Buddhas appear in the world for a great cause: [sharing] Buddha’s knowledge.’

世人外迷着相，内迷着空；若能于相离相、于空离空，即是内外不迷。若悟此法，一念心开，是为开佛知见。
“The deluded are attached to existence and non-existence; when they are free from these, things are cognized but not grasped, and delusion will disappear. When this teaching dawns on you, your mind will be transformed. This is called accessing the Buddha’s knowledge.

佛，犹觉也。分为四门，开觉知见、示觉知见、悟觉知见、入觉知见。若闻开示，便能悟入，即觉知见，本来真性而得出现。

“Buddha means the awakened. The knowledge of the awakened is accessible through understanding and realizing. Once you have understood [Intrinsic Nature], you can realize it. This is called having the knowledge of the awakened or revealing the original true nature.

汝慎勿错解经意，见他道：开示悟入，自是佛之知见。我辈无分。若作此解，乃是谤经毁佛也。彼既是佛，已具知见，何用更开？汝今当信，佛知见者，只汝自心，更无别佛。盖为一切众生，自蔽光明，贪爱尘境，外缘内扰，甘受驱驰。便劳他世尊，从三昧起，种种苦口，劝令寝息，莫向外求，与佛无二。故云：开佛知见。

“Don’t misinterpret ‘understanding and realizing’ in the scripture. Don’t say that it is buddhas, not people like us, who have that knowledge. Otherwise, you do a disservice to buddhas and sutras. For buddhas, who are endowed with perfect knowledge, there is nothing more to know. You must know that the Buddha’s knowledge only lies within rather than somewhere else. The inner light of the sentient beings is veiled by their cravings, and their mind is disturbed and enslaved by external conditions and defilements within. To help them overcome their desire and attachment to external objects, Buddha had to come out of Samādhi and take the role of a patient teacher. In this way, they can be on a par with buddhas. This is ‘accessing the Buddha’s knowledge’.

吾亦劝一切人，于自心中，常开佛之知见。世人心邪，愚迷造罪，口善心恶，贪瞋嫉妒，谄佞我慢，侵人害物，自开众生知见。若能正心，常生智慧，观照自心，止恶行善，是自开佛之知见。
"I also encourage people to access the Buddha's knowledge from within. [However,] with distorted perception and false views, the deluded people in the world commit wrongdoings. They speak something good while harboring something evil. They are greedy, hateful, jealous, flattering, deceitful, arrogant, and harmful. If they rectify their views, develop wisdom, observe their mind, discard the unwholesome and cultivate the wholesome, they can access the Buddha's knowledge.

汝须念念开佛知见，勿开众生知见。开佛知见，即是出世；开众生知见，即是世间。汝若但劳劳执念，以为功课者，何异牦牛爱尾。
"At any time, access the Buddha's knowledge instead of the perception of sentient beings. The Buddha's knowledge is supramundane while the perception of sentient beings is mundane. If you completely focus on chanting, you are like the yak that only cares about its tail [rather than its life]."

达曰：若然者，但得解义，不劳诵经耶？
Fada asked, "Does that mean there is no need to chant as long as I understand it?"

师曰：经有何过，岂障汝念？只为迷悟在人，损益由己。口诵心行，即是转经；口诵心不行，即是被经转。听吾偈曰：

The Master replied, “Well, there is nothing wrong with chanting. The problem is whether you understand it or not. If you understand it, chanting will be beneficial; otherwise, it’ll be detrimental. Chanted with contemplation, the sutra will be edifying; without contemplation, the sutra will impede you. Please listen to this poem:

心迷法华转，心悟转法华。
诵经久不明，与义作仇家。
无念念即正，有念念成邪。
有无俱不计，长御白牛车。

“A deluded mind will be impeded by the sutra;
An awakened mind will be edified by the sutra.
Chanting the sutra mechanically for a long time,
You end up being ignorant of its meaning.
Chanting it without a judging mind is correct;
Chanting it with a judging mind is wrong.
If you are attached to neither,
You are [heading for liberation] on the white-ox wagon①.”

达闻偈，不觉悲泣，言下大悟，而告师曰：法达从昔已来，实未曾转法华，乃被法华转。再启曰：经云：诸大声闻乃至菩萨，皆尽思共度量，不能测佛智。今令凡夫但悟自心，便名佛之知见。自非上根，未免疑谤。又经说三车，羊鹿牛车与白牛之车，如何区别？愿和尚再垂开示。

---

① The white-ox wagon in the *Lotus Sutra* refers to the supreme vehicle.

Upon hearing this poem, Fada gained a profound insight and told the Master in tears, "I have always been impeded by the sutra but never edified by it." He raised another question, "The sutra says, 'Even with all their thoughts and speculations, sages like Voice-hearers and Bodhisattvas cannot fathom the wisdom of Buddha.' Nevertheless, as long as ordinary beings realize their original mind, they have access to the Buddha's knowledge. Yet, those who are not endowed with superior faculties may doubt the sutra, thereby doing a disservice to it. In the sutra, there are three wagons drawn by the goat, the deer, and the ox. How do they differ from the one drawn by the white ox? Master, please instruct me."

师曰：经意分明，汝自迷背。诸三乘人，不能测佛智者，患在度量也。饶伊尽思共推，转加悬远。佛本为凡夫说，不为佛说。此理若不肯信者，从他退席。殊不知，坐却白牛车，更于门外觅三车。况经文明向汝道：唯一佛乘，无有余乘。若二若三乃至无数方便，种种因缘譬喻言词，是法皆为一佛乘故。汝何不省，三车是假，为昔时故；一乘是实，为今时故。只教汝去假归实，归实之后，实亦无名。应知所有珍财，尽属于汝，由汝受用，更不作父想，亦不作子想，亦无用想。是名持《法华经》，从劫至劫，手不释卷，从昼至夜，无不念时也。

The Master said, "The meaning is quite clear. [You don't understand it because] you are deluded. It is exactly their speculation that prevents disciples of the three vehicles from fathoming the wisdom of Buddha. The more they think, the further they go astray. What Buddha taught is for ordinary beings instead of the awakened ones. [In the sutra,] those who didn't believe this [one-vehicle] teaching left the lecture. They left because they were still seeking the other three vehicles outside the gate despite that they were already in the white-ox wagon [—the only wagon available]. Moreover, the sutra reads 'The Buddha vehicle is the only vehicle available; there are no other vehicles.' The two or three vehicles, like many other parables, are all expedient teachings for the sake of one-vehicle—the Buddha vehicle. Just accept it that 'three wagons' is expedient. Ultimately, there is only one. You are supposed to put aside the expedient and go directly for the ultimate, and even transcend the 'ultimate' afterwards. You must know that all treasures [mentioned in the sutra] are for you to enjoy; however, you should never cling to the concepts of father, son, or enjoyment. Only in this way can you chant the *Lotus Sutra* properly, and you should do it day and night."

达蒙启发，踊跃欢喜，以偈赞曰：

Fada was inspired by the instruction and overwhelmed with joy. He also made a poem in praise of the Master's teaching:

经诵三千部，曹溪一句亡，
未明出世旨，宁歇累生狂。
羊鹿牛权设，初中后善扬，
谁知火宅内，元是法中王。

"Although for three thousand times I have chanted,
My way of chanting was disapproved by a few words of the Master in Caoxi.

Without knowing the supramundane purpose of the sutra,
How can one put an end to his arrogance accumulated for lives?
The goat, deer, and ox wagons,
Are expedient teachings.
Those trapped in the house on fire[①]
Are actually the kings of Dharma[②]."

师曰：汝今后方可名念经僧也。达从此领玄旨，亦不辍诵经。

The Master said, "From now on, you are a monk who truly knows how to chant sutras." Having received the profound teaching, Fada kept chanting the Sutra as instructed.

僧智通，寿州安丰人。初看《楞伽经》。约千余遍，而不会三身四智。礼师求解其义。

Zhitong, a monk from Anfeng, Shouzhou, couldn't understand Three Bodies and Four Knowledges in the *Laṅkāvatāra Sutra* even after reading it for more than one thousand times. So he came to the Master for an explanation.

师曰：三身者，清净法身，汝之性也；圆满报身，汝之智也；千百亿化身，汝之行也。若离本性，别说三身，即名有身无智；若悟三身无有自性，即名四智菩提。听吾偈曰：

The Master said, "The Pure Dharma-body is your nature; the Perfect

---

① The house on fire: The cycle of birth-and-death.

② The kings of Dharma: buddhas.

Enjoyment-body your Knowledge; the Infinite Manifestation-bodies your actions. These are the Three Bodies. Without the original nature, the Three Bodies you talk about will be reduced to something called Bodies without Knowledges. If you understand the emptiness of the Three Bodies, you will obtain the Four Knowledges of Bodhi. Listen to my poem:

自性具三身，发明成四智，
不离见闻缘，超然登佛地。
吾今为汝说，谛信永无迷，
莫学驰求者，终日说菩提。

"Intrinsic Nature is endowed with Three Bodies.
When Intrinsic Nature is realized, Four Knowledges will be acquired.
Through what you cognize,
Buddha-stage can be reached immediately.
Put faith in my words,
So that you will never get deluded.
Do not follow those who seek externally
And those who merely talk about Bodhi all day long."

通再启曰：四智之义，可得闻乎？师曰：既会三身，便明四智。何更问耶？若离三身，别谈四智，此名有智无身。即此有智，还成无智。

Zhitong continued, "May I know the meaning of Four Knowledges?" The Master replied, "Why bother? Once Three Bodies are understood, the meaning of Four Knowledges will come to you naturally. Without

Three Bodies, the Four Knowledges you talk about will be reduced to Non-knowledge, which is called Knowledges without Bodies."

复说偈曰：
The Master came up with another poem:

大圆镜智性清净，平等性智心无病，
妙观察智见非功，成所作智同圆镜。
五八六七果因转，但用名言无实性，
若于转处不留情，繁兴永处那伽定。

"The Knowledge of Perfect Mirror leads to pure nature,
The Knowledge of Sameness an undefiled mind.
The Knowledge of Marvelous Observation works without effort.
The Knowledge of Accomplishment [works]
In the way a mirror [reflects].
When consciousnesses are transformed into Knowledges,
Only their names, not their substance, are changed.
When consciousnesses are transformed completely,
You will always be in Naga Samādhi.

如上转识为智也。教中云，转前五识为成所作智，转第六识为妙观察智，转第七识为平等性智，转第八识为大圆镜智。虽六七因中转，五八果上转，但转其名而不转其体也。
"That is transforming consciousnesses into Knowledges. According to the doctrine, the first five consciousnesses (i.e. the physical senses) are transformed into the Knowledge of Accomplishment, the sixth

consciousness (i.e. the conscious mind) into the Knowledge of Marvelous Observation, the seventh consciousness (i.e. the egoic mind) into the Knowledge of Sameness, the eighth consciousness (i.e. the subconscious mind) into the Knowledge of Perfect Mirror. The sixth and seventh consciousnesses are transformed at the initial stage while the first to the fifth as well as the eighth consciousnesses are transformed at the final stage. Although they are transformed, it is their names, not their substance, that are changed."

通顿悟性智，遂呈偈曰：

Zhitong immediately understood the teaching and put his insight in a poem:

三身元我体，四智本心明，
身智融无碍，应物任随形。
起修皆妄动，守住匪真精，
妙旨因师晓，终亡染污名。

"My body is just Three Bodies,
And my mind is no other than Four Knowledges.
Bodies and Knowledges are in perfect harmony,
And manifest themselves to suit the conditions.
Deliberate practice is wrong.
Idleness is not desirable either.
The wonderful Knowledge is revealed through the Master's teaching,
So all designations and defilements are abandoned at last."

僧智常，信州贵溪人，髫年出家，志求见性。一日参礼。师问曰：汝从何来？欲求何事？

Venerable Zhichang, a native of Guixi in Xinzhou, joined the monastic order when he was a child and resolved to realize Intrinsic Nature. One day he paid a visit [in homage to] the Master. The Master asked him, "Where are you from? What do you want from me?"

曰：学人近往洪州白峰山礼大通和尚，蒙示见性成佛之义。未决狐疑，远来投礼，伏望和尚慈悲指示。

Zhichang replied, "I just came from Mount Baifeng in Hongzhou, where I received instructions on realizing Intrinsic Nature from Most Venerable Datong. However, I still have doubts, so I come all the way to pay homage to you, hoping that you can teach me."

师曰：彼有何言句？汝试举看。曰：智常到彼，凡经三月，未蒙示诲。为法切故，一夕独入丈室，请问：如何是某甲本心本性？

The Master asked, "What instructions did you receive? Tell me some." Zhichang replied, "I hadn't received any for about three months since I arrived there. Being so eager to hear Dharma, I went to the abbot's room one night and asked, 'What is my original mind?'

大通乃曰：汝见虚空否？

"Datong then told me, 'Have you seen the space?'

对曰：见。

"I said, 'Yes, I have.'

彼曰：汝见虚空有相貌否？
"Datong asked, 'Does it have any appearance? '

对曰：虚空无形，有何相貌？
"I replied, 'Since it is formless, how can it have any appearance?'

彼曰：汝之本性，犹如虚空，了无一物可见，是名正见；无一物可知，是名真知。无有青黄长短，但见本源清净，觉体圆明，即名见性成佛，亦名如来知见。学人虽闻此说，犹未决了，乞和尚开示。
Datong said, 'Just like the space, your original nature is empty. You have the right view if you realize that there is nothing to be seen in it; you have the true knowledge if you realize that there is nothing to be known in it. When there is no conceptualization in terms of color or shape, the pure origin and the perfect clear awareness will appear. This is called "having realized Intrinsic Nature and attained Buddhahood", also known as the "Buddha's knowledge". ' Having heard this teaching, however, I'm still confused. Please give me your instruction."

师曰：彼师所说，犹存见知，故令汝未了。吾今示汝一偈：
The Master replied, "Based on what your previous master said, he still seemed to be attached to views and knowledge. So his teaching left you in confusion. Now, I give you a poem:

不见一法存无见，大似浮云遮日面，
不知一法守空知，还如太虚生闪电。

此之知见瞥然兴，错认何曾解方便，
汝当一念自知非，自己灵光常显现。

"The attachment to the view that there is nothing to be seen
Is like the cloud that veils the sun.
The attachment to the knowledge that there is nothing to be known
Is like a lightning flash from nowhere.
Such views are expedient concepts.
If you take the expedient as the ultimate, you are going nowhere.
Once you realize it's wrong to take it that way,
Your spiritual light starts to shine."

常闻偈已，心意豁然。乃述偈曰：

Having heard the poem, Zhichang grasped it immediately, and replied with his poem:

无端起知见，着相求菩提，
情存一念悟，宁越昔时迷。
自性觉源体，随照枉迁流，
不入祖师室，茫然趣两头。

"With incorrect views from nowhere,
I seek Bodhi through forms.
As long as the enlightenment remains conceptualized,
It is impossible to dispel the delusion in the past.
Intrinsic Nature is the origin of awakening.
[Instead of the origin,] I follow in vain what it gives rise to.
Had it not been for your [correct] instruction,

I would have been misled by the two concepts."

智常一日问师曰：佛说三乘法，又言最上乘。弟子未解，愿为教授。
One day, Zhichang asked the Master, "Buddha taught three vehicles, but he later mentioned another one—the supreme vehicle. I don't understand. Could you please clarify it?"

师曰：汝观自本心，莫着外法相。法无四乘，人心自有等差。见闻转诵是小乘；悟法解义是中乘；依法修行是大乘；万法尽通，万法俱备，一切不染，离诸法相，一无所得，名最上乘。乘是行义，不在口争。汝须自修，莫问吾也。一切时中，自性自如。
The Master said, "You should observe your own original mind. Don't get attached to external forms. Dharma is not to be divided into four vehicles, but it appears to be so because people have different levels of understanding. Those who merely receive and pass on Dharma verbally are of the small vehicle; those who understand the meaning, the middle vehicle; those who practice accordingly, the great vehicle. Such is the state of the supreme vehicle: everything is connected and available while nothing causes defilements, attachment, or the illusion of gaining. This vehicle is about practice rather than arguing. You should get the answer through your own practice. Don't ask me. Stay with Intrinsic Nature all the time and don't get disturbed."

常礼谢执侍，终师之世。
Out of gratitude, Zhichang devoted himself to serving the Master. His service continued until the Master passed away.

僧志道，广州南海人也。请益曰：学人自出家，览《涅槃经》十载有余，未明大意，愿和尚垂诲。

[One day,] Venerable Zhidao, from Nanhai, Guangzhou, asked the Master, “Since the beginning of my monkhood, I have been reading the *Mahāparinirvāṇa Sutra*. It has been more than ten years, but I still don’t understand its general idea. Could you please teach me?”

师曰：汝何处未明？

The Master replied, “What confuses you?”

曰：诸行无常，是生灭法；生灭灭已，寂灭为乐。于此疑惑。

The monk answered, “Everything that is conditioned is impermanent and hence subject to arising and ceasing. When there is no arising and ceasing, there is the happiness of Cessation (i.e. Nirvana). This confuses me.”

师曰：汝作么生疑？

The Master said, “How does it confuse you?”

曰：一切众生皆有二身，谓色身、法身也。色身无常，有生有灭；法身有常，无知无觉。经云：“生灭灭已，寂灭为乐”者，不审何身寂灭？何身受乐？若色身者，色身灭时，四大分散，全然是苦，苦不可言乐。若法身寂灭，即同草木瓦石，谁当受乐？又法性是生灭之体，五蕴是生灭之用，一体五用，生灭是常。生则从体起用，灭则摄用归体。若听更生，即有情之类，不断不灭；若不听更生，则永归寂灭，同于无情之物。如是，则一切诸法被涅槃之所禁伏，尚不得生，何乐之有？

Zhidao replied, “Every being has two bodies: the physical body and the Dharma-body. The physical body is impermanent and hence subject to arising and ceasing. The Dharma-body is permanent without perception or sensation. The Sutra says, ‘If there is no arising and ceasing, happiness of Cessation is attained.’ I don’t know which body attains Cessation and which enjoys the happiness. If it were the physical body, there would be no happiness at the extremely painful moment when the body ceases to function and the four elements start to disintegrate. If it were the Dharma-body, no body would enjoy happiness. It is because this body, upon Cessation, would be like plants and rocks which have no sentience. What’s more, for arising and ceasing, Dharma nature is its essence, and Five Aggregates are its functions. Since this one [permanent] essence is connected with five functions, it follows that arising and ceasing should be permanent [too]. Functions arise from the essence; when they cease, they return to the essence. If they were to arise again, sentient beings would not perish. If they were not to arise again, they would be in the state of Cessation forever and would be the same as the non-sentient. Consequently, everything would be prevented by Nirvana from coming into being. How can you call that happiness?”

师曰：汝是释子，何习外道断常邪见，而议最上乘法？据汝所说，即色身外别有法身，离生灭求于寂灭。又推涅槃常乐，言有身受用。斯乃执吝生死，耽着世乐。汝今当知，佛为一切迷人，认五蕴和合为自体相，分别一切法为外尘相，好生恶死，念念迁流，不知梦幻虚假，枉受轮回。以常乐涅槃翻为苦相，终日驰求。佛愍此故，乃示涅槃真乐。刹那无有生相，刹那无有灭相，更无生灭可灭，是则寂灭现前。当现前时，亦无现前之量，乃谓常乐。此乐无有受者，亦无不受者，岂有一体五用之名？何况更言涅槃禁伏诸法，令永不生。斯乃谤佛毁法。听吾偈曰：

The Master said, "As a disciple of Buddha, how can you listen to the heretical eternalists and annihilationists and make such speculations about the supreme Dharma? If what you said were correct, there would be a Dharma-body independent from the physical one as well as Cessation apart from the arising and ceasing. Again, you speculate that there is a body that can enjoy the eternal happiness of Nirvana. This is because you are still clinging to life and indulging in worldly pleasures. You must know that the deluded identify the combination of Five Aggregates as self and treat everything else as external objects, so they crave for life and loathe death. Such mentality flows like an unceasing stream. Also, unaware of the illusory and dream-like nature [of all phenomena], they are trapped in the cycle of birth-and-death. And they perversely take Nirvana—the eternal happiness—for suffering, so they seek for [worldly pleasures] all the time. Buddha understood this fact, so out of compassion he used his Nirvana—the true happiness—as expedient means. In each moment, there is no arising, no ceasing, and no arising-and-ceasing to be extinguished. This state, whose presence cannot be measured, is Cessation, also known as eternal happiness. There is neither someone nor no one experiencing such happiness, so 'one essence with five functions' is nothing but a misconception. Even worse is the misunderstanding that 'Nirvana prevents everything from arising forever'; this is a disservice to Buddha and Dharma. Now listen to my poem:

无上大涅槃，圆明常寂照，
凡愚谓之死，外道执为断，
诸求二乘人，目以为无作，
尽属情所计，六十二见本。
妄立虚假名，何为真实义，
惟有过量人，通达无取舍。
以知五蕴法，及以蕴中我，
外现众色象，一一音声相，
平等如梦幻，不起凡圣见，
不作涅槃解，二边三际断。
常应诸根用，而不起用想，
分别一切法，不起分别想。
劫火烧海底，风鼓山相击，
真常寂灭乐，涅槃相如是。
吾今强言说，令汝舍邪见，
汝勿随言解，许汝知少分。

"Always illuminating in silence,
The supreme Nirvana is perfect and clear.
The deluded mistake it for death;
The heretics take it for annihilation;
Those of the two [non-great] vehicles
Mistakenly regard it to be inactive.

These misconceptions are based on discrimination,
And they give rise to the sixty-two false views.
These misconceptions are nothing but provisional terms,
So by no means they are the ultimate truth.
Only those with great wisdom can understand Nirvana,
In which there is nothing to gain and nothing to lose.
They know that Five Aggregates,
'I' superimposed thereon,
And external phenomena,
Such as images and sounds
Have the same nature as dreams and illusion.
Also they don't discriminate between sages and the ordinary.
They don't conceptualize Nirvana,
So they are not bound by Two Extreme Views① or time②
Their faculties function normally,
While there is no conceptualization of that process.
Their mind discriminates things,
While there is no conceptualization of that process.
Even when the entire ocean dries up in the apocalyptic fire,
And mountains collide in the disastrous storm,
The true and permanent happiness of Cessation remains undisturbed.
This is what Nirvana is like.
Despite the difficulty, I have explained what is inexplicable,

---

① Two Extreme Views: Eternalism and Annihilationism

② Time: The past, present, and future

So that you can abandon false views.
If you don’t stick to my words literally,
I will admit that you catch a glimpse of Dharma.”

志道闻偈大悟，踊跃作礼而退。
On hearing the poem, Zhidao gained a profound insight. Then he thanked the Master and left.

行思禅师，生吉州安城刘氏。闻曹溪法席盛化，径来参礼，遂问曰：当何所务，即不落阶级？
Xingsi, a Chan master born in a Liu’s family in Ancheng, Jizhou, came to pay a visit at the news of a good popular Dharma master here in Caoxi. He asked the Master, “In what way can I go without stages [so as to attain sudden enlightenment]?”

师曰：汝曾作什么来？
The Master replied, “What have you been practicing?”

曰：圣谛亦不为。
Xingsi answered, “Nothing. I don’t even aim at the ultimate truth.”

师曰：落何阶级？
The Master asked, “Your progress?”

曰：圣谛尚不为，何阶级之有？
Xingsi replied, “The ultimate truth has nothing to do with progress.

Why bother bringing up progress?"

师深器之，令思首众。一日，师谓曰：汝当分化一方，无令断绝。
The Master was deeply impressed so he let Xingsi lead the monks. One day, The Master told him, "You should pass on our tradition somewhere so as to maintain the lineage."

思既得法，遂回吉州青原山，弘法绍化（谥弘济禅师）。
Having inherited the lineage, Xingsi went back to Mount Qingyuan in Jizhou and started teaching there. He was posthumously known as Chan Master Hongji.

怀让禅师，金州杜氏子也。初谒嵩山安国师，安发之曹溪参叩。让至礼拜。
Chan Master Huairang, the son of the Du family in Jinzhou, received instructions from the Imperial Preceptor An at Mount Song, who later advised him to seek further instructions in Caoxi. Huairang came and paid homage to Master Huineng.

师曰：甚处来？
The Master asked, "Where did you come from?"

曰：嵩山。
Huairang answered, "From Mount Song."

师曰：什么物？恁么来？

The Master continued, "What is the thing? By what did it come?"

曰：说似一物即不中。
He answered, "You miss it when you describe it."

师曰：还可修证否？
The Master asked, "Is further cultivation needed?"

曰：修证即不无，污染即不得。
He replied, "Cultivation is not unnecessary, but defilements are not to be accumulated."

师曰：只此不污染，诸佛之所护念。汝既如是，吾亦如是。西天般若多罗谶，汝足下出一马驹，踏杀天下人。应在汝心，不须速说。
The Master said, "It is the only thing that is free from defilements and guarded by buddhas. It is attained by both you and me. Master Prajñātāra in India predicted that you will have a disciple who will destroy the delusion of many in a way a horse tramples enemies to death. Keep it to yourself until the day comes."

让豁然契会，遂执侍左右一十五载，日臻玄奥。后往南岳，大阐禅宗，敕谥大慧禅师。
Huairang got it right away. Then, he served the Master for 15 years, during which he got closer and closer to the truth. Later, he went to Mount Heng in the South and spread the Chan teaching there. After his death, the emperor bestowed upon him the posthumous title "Chan

Master Dahui".

永嘉玄觉禅师，温州戴氏子。少习经论，精天台止观法门。因看《维摩经》发明心地。

Xuanjue, a Chan master from Yongjia and a son of Dai's family in Wenzhou, was well-versed in scriptures in his youth, and he was also an expert in meditation—tranquility and insight—of Tiantai School. He came to understand the original mind after reading the *Vimalakīrti Sutra*.

偶师弟子玄策相访，与其剧谈，出言暗合诸祖。策云：仁者得法师谁？

One day, Xuance, one of the Master's disciples visited and had a discussion with Xuanjue. In their discussion, he found what Xuanjue said was consistent with patriarchs' words, so he asked, "Who is your teacher?"

曰：我听方等经论，各有师承。后于《维摩经》悟佛心宗，未有证明者。

Xuanjue replied, "I heard that Mahayana teachings are passed on through teachers in their own lineages, but I understood Buddha's teaching on [the original] mind by reading *Vimalakīrti Sutra*. However, this realization has not been verified by anyone."

策云：威音王已前即得，威音王已后，无师自悟，尽是天然外道。

Xuance said, "It is possible for someone to realize the Truth by himself prior to the time of the first Buddha in the previous era. After that, however, anyone who claims such realization is no more than a heretic."

曰：愿仁者为我证据。
Xuanjue requested, "Could you please verify my realization?"

策云：我言轻。曹溪有六祖大师，四方云集，并是受法者。若去，则与偕行。
Xuance replied, "I am not qualified. In Caoxi, the Sixth Patriarch Huineng is attracting Dharma-seekers from everywhere. I can take you there if you want."

觉遂同策来参。绕师三匝，振锡而立。
Xuanjue agreed. He met the Master and circumambulated him three times. Then, he stopped and made a heavy thump with his staff striking the ground.

师曰：夫沙门者，具三千威仪，八万细行。大德自何方而来，生大我慢？
The Master said, "As a monk, you should not forget your manners. What makes you so arrogant?"

觉曰：生死事大，无常迅速。
Xuanjue replied, "Forget about manners. Life and death matters; impermanence strikes fast."

师曰：何不体取无生，了无速乎？
The Master asked, "Why not experience what is beyond life and realize what is beyond time?"

曰：体即无生，了本无速。
Xuanjue replied, "Experience and realize it, you will find that it is beyond life and time."

师曰：如是！如是！
The Master said, "Exactly! Exactly!"

玄觉方具威仪礼拜，须臾告辞。
Xuanjue then paid homage again, but this time in a proper manner. Shortly, he was ready to leave.

师曰：返太速乎？
The Master said, "Why the hurry? You've been here just for a short time."

曰：本自非动，岂有速耶？
Xuanjue replied, "It does not move in the first place, so the concept of time, even a short period, does not apply."

师曰：谁知非动？
The Master asked, "Who knows that it does not move?"

曰：仁者自生分别。

Xuanjue answered, “That is the result of your discrimination.”

师曰：汝甚得无生之意。

The Master said, “You have really penetrated the meaning of what is beyond life.”

曰：无生岂有意耶？

Xuanjue replied, “Does what is beyond life have meaning?”

师曰：无意谁当分别？

The Master continued, “Without meaning, how can discrimination take place?”

曰：分别亦非意。

Xuanjue replied, “Even discrimination is beyond meaning.”

师曰：善哉！少留一宿。

The Master said, “Good. Please stay for one night.”

时谓一宿觉，后著《证道歌》盛行于世。谥曰无相大师，时称为真觉焉。

Thus, Xuanjue was called “Yixiu Jue (awakened overnight) ”. Later, he wrote a poem on realizing Intrinsic Nature, which became quite popular. After his death, he was called “Master Wuxiang (formless) ” and also “Zhenjue (the truly awakened) ”.

禅者智隍，初参五祖，自谓已得正受。庵居长坐，积二十年。
Zhihuang, a meditator, thought that he had attained deep concentration after he visited the Fifth Patriarch. He had been practicing sitting meditation in a hut for twenty years.

师弟子玄策，游方至河朔，闻隍之名，造庵问云：汝在此作什么？
The Master's disciple Xuance, in the trip to Heshuo, heard about him, so Xuance visited the hut and asked him, "What are you doing here?"

隍曰：入定。
Zhihuang answered, "I am cultivating concentration."

策云：汝云入定，为有心入耶？无心入耶？若无心入者，一切无情草木瓦石，应合得定；若有心入者，一切有情含识之流，亦应得定。
Xuance continued, "Does your mind exist in your concentrated state? If it doesn't, then all non-sentient beings such as weeds, trees, and rocks should all be in the same state you are in. If it does, all sentient beings should be in the same state you are in."

隍曰：我正入定时，不见有"有无"之心。
Zhihuang replied, "Neither. In my concentrated state, I don't pay attention to whether the mind exists or not."

策云：不见有"有无"之心，即是常定，何有出入？若有出入，即非大定。

Xuance asked, "If that is the case, you should always stay in that state. How is it possible to get 'into' or 'out of' the state? If there is 'into' or 'out of', this state is not the supreme concentration then."

隍无对。良久，问曰：师嗣谁耶？

After a long silence, Zhihuang asked, "Who is your teacher?"

策云：我师曹溪六祖。

Xuance answered, "My teacher is the Sixth Patriarch in Caoxi."

隍云：六祖以何为禅定？

Zhihuang continued, "According to the Sixth Patriarch, what is concentration?"

策云：我师所说，妙湛圆寂，体用如如。五阴本空，六尘非有；不出不入，不定不乱，禅性无住，离住禅寂，禅性无生，离生禅想；心如虚空，亦无虚空之量。

Xuance answered, "According to my teacher, it is an extraordinary and pure state that is perfect and peaceful. In this state, the essence and the function are unified and undisturbed. Five Aggregates and Six Objects are of empty nature and intrinsically non-existent; there is no discrimination between entering and exiting, focusing and distraction. The nature of this concentration does not dwell on anything, so there is no clinging to the sense of stillness; its nature is beyond arising and cessation, so there is no intention to attain the concentration. The mind [in this state] is like the boundless space but is beyond the concept of dimension."

隍闻是说，径来谒师。

Upon hearing these words, Zhihuang came to visit the Master right away.

师问云：仁者何来？

The Master asked him, "Why are you here?"

隍具述前缘。

He explained everything.

师云：诚如所言，汝但心如虚空，不着空见；应用无碍，动静无心；凡圣情忘，能所俱泯；性相如如，无不定时也。

The Master said, "Just as Xuance told you, you should keep your mind as empty as the space without clinging to the view of emptiness. Your mind should function freely without being attached to any state, dynamic or static; eliminate the duality: the ordinary and the sages, the cognizer and the cognized. When the nature and the form therefrom are unified, you will always be in the concentration."

隍于是大悟。二十年所得心，都无影响。其夜河北士庶闻空中有声云：隍禅师今日得道。隍后礼辞，复归河北，开化四众。

These words struck Zhihuang enlightened, sweeping away all concepts he had gained in the past twenty years. At that night, people in

Hebei[1] heard a voice from the sky, "Chan Master Zhihuang attained enlightenment today." Having thanked the Master, Zhihuang left for Hebei and started teaching there.

一僧问师曰：黄梅意旨甚么人得？
A monk came and asked the Master, "Who received the teaching [from the Fifth Patriarch] in Huangmei?"

师云：会佛法人得。
The Master answered, "The one that knows Dharma."

僧云：和尚还得否？
The monk said, "Is that you?"

师云：我不会佛法。
The Master replied, " [No, not me.] I don't know Dharma."

师一日欲濯所授之衣，而无美泉。因至寺后五里许，见山林郁茂，瑞气盘旋。师振锡卓地，泉应手而出，积以为池。乃跪膝浣衣石上。
One day, the Master wanted to wash the robe he inherited but could not find a clean spring nearby, so he went to the place about five-*li* (about 2.7 km) away behind the temple, where he saw auspicious signs: thriving bushes and rising clouds. He then hit the ground with his staff. Immediately, water welled up, forming a pond. By the pond, he knelt

---

① Hebei: The area where Zhihuang's hut is.

down to wash the robe on a rock.

忽有一僧来礼拜云：方辩是西蜀人。昨于南天竺国，见达摩大师，嘱方辩速往唐土。吾传大迦叶正法眼藏及僧伽梨，见传六代，于韶州曹溪，汝去瞻礼。方辩远来，愿见我师传来衣钵。

At that moment, a monk came to pay homage to the Master and said, "I am Fangbian from a place to the west of Shu①. I met Master Bodhidharma in South India the other day, and he told me to come to China as soon as possible. He said, 'It has been six generations since I brought Mahakashapa's teachings and robe to China. Now they are in Caoxi, Shaozhou. You should make a pilgrimage there.' I have come all the way here in the hope of seeing that robe."

师乃出示，次问：上人攻何事业？

The Master showed him the robe and asked, "What are you good at? "

曰：善塑。

He answered, "Making statues."

师正色曰：汝试塑看。

With a serious look, the Master said, "Try to make one then."

辩罔措。过数日，塑就真相，可高七寸，曲尽其妙。

Although Fangbian was puzzled by the request, several days later, he

---

① Shu: Now Sichuan Province.

made a lifelike statue, seven-*cun* (about 23cm) in height.

师笑曰：汝只解塑性，不解佛性。
The Master laughed, "You may know how to make Buddha statues, but you don't know Buddha Nature."

师舒手摩方辩顶曰：永为人天福田。
With his hand on the head of Fangbian, the Master said, "Still, this statue can produce merit for human and celestial beings forever."

师仍以衣酬之。
The Master gave him a robe as a reward.

辩取衣分为三：一披塑像，一自留，一用棕裹瘗地中。誓曰：后得此衣，乃吾出世，住持于此，重建殿宇。（宋嘉祐八年，有僧惟先，修殿掘地，得衣如新。像在高泉寺，祈祷辄应。）
Fangbian took the robe and divided it into three: one used to cover the statue, one kept for himself, and the last one wrapped in a palm leaf and buried. Then he took a vow, "The next time I get this robe is the time I get reborn here as the abbot and rebuild the monastery". (In 1063 AD, during the reconstruction, a monk called Weixian unearthed the robe fragment, still fresh and new. As for the statue, it was later enshrined in Gaoquan Temple. It did bring merits to whoever prays to it.)

有僧举卧轮禅师偈云：
There was a monk reciting a poem by the Chan master Wolun:

卧轮有伎俩，能断百思想。
对境心不起，菩提日日长。

"Wolun has a knack
In cutting off all thoughts.
Upon objects, no thoughts arise.
Day by day, his Bodhi grows."

师闻之，曰：此偈未明心地。若依而行之，是加系缚。

Hearing it, the Master commented, "This poem shows that its author hasn't realized the original mind. It will only bring additional fetters to whoever practices accordingly."

因示一偈曰：

In response, he composed a poem:

惠能没伎俩，
不断百思想。
对境心数起，
菩提作么长。

"Huineng has no knack,
In cutting off thoughts.
Upon objects, his thoughts often arise.
How can his Bodhi grow?"

顿渐品第八
Chapter 8
On Sudden and Gradual Teachings

时，祖师居曹溪宝林，神秀大师在荆南玉泉寺。于时两宗盛化，人皆称南能北秀，故有南北二宗顿渐之分。而学者莫知宗趣。

At that time, our Master was residing at Baolin Temple in Caoxi and Master Shenxiu was at Yuquan Temple in Jingnan[1]. Both schools were popular, thus the saying "the Huineng's Sudden Teaching in the south and Shenxiu's Gradual Teaching in the north". However, Dharma learners don't know their difference.

师谓众曰：法本一宗，人有南北；法即一种，见有迟疾。何名顿渐？法无顿渐，人有利钝，故名顿渐。

The Master then told everyone that, "Originally, there is only one Dharma and one teaching, but people with different backgrounds may progress at different paces on their awakening journey. Then why is the teaching divided? The teaching itself is neither sudden nor gradual, but it is perceived so by practitioners of different faculties: Sudden

---

① Jingnan: Now in Hubei Province.

Teaching for the sharp and Gradual Teaching for the dull."

然秀之徒众，往往讥南宗祖师不识一字，有何所长？秀曰：他得无师之智，深悟上乘，吾不如也。且吾师五祖，亲传衣法，岂徒然哉？吾恨不能远去亲近，虚受国恩。汝等诸人，毋滞于此，可往曹溪参决。

However, Shenxiu's disciples often teased Master Huineng about his illiteracy and questioned his ability. Shenxiu told them, "Huineng has realized the Truth by himself and understood the teaching of the supreme vehicle. I am no match for him. It is quite reasonable for my master, the Fifth Patriarch, to give the robe and the teaching to him. It's a pity that I could not visit him in person due to my commitment to the royal family. Don't stay here. Go to Caoxi for instructions."

一日，命门人志诚曰：汝聪明多智，可为吾到曹溪听法。若有所闻，尽心记取，还为吾说。志诚禀命至曹溪，随众参请，不言来处。时，祖师告众曰：今有盗法之人，潜在此会。志诚即出礼拜，具陈其事。

One day, he told one of his disciples Zhicheng, "You are intelligent, so you may go to Caoxi for Dharma talks. Try to remember what you hear and tell me when you come back." As ordered, Zhicheng went to Caoxi and joined the audience without disclosing where he came from. At that moment, the Master told the audience, "One of you came today with an ulterior motive." Immediately, Zhicheng came forward, paid homage, and explained himself.

师曰：汝从玉泉来，应是细作。

Then the Master spoke to him, "You come from Yuquan Temple as a spy."

对曰：不是。

He replied, "No, I am not."

师曰：何得不是？

The Master continued, "How is that?"

对曰：未说即是，说了不是。

He answered, "How can someone be a spy when his identity is disclosed?"

师曰：汝师若为示众？

The Master asked, "What did you learn from your teacher?"

对曰：常指诲大众，住心观静，长坐不卧。

He replied, "To focus on the stillness of the mind by sitting for a long time without lying down."

师曰：住心观静，是病非禅；长坐拘身，于理何益？听吾偈曰：

The Master said, "Focusing on the stillness of the mind is a wrong practice, not Chan. How can long sitting benefit you? Now listen to my poem:

生来坐不卧，死去卧不坐；
一具臭骨头，何为立功课？
"Whether in a sitting position while alive
Or in a lying position while dead,
Our body is nothing more than a husk,
So it is of no significance in your daily practice."

志诚再拜曰：弟子在秀大师处学道九年，不得契悟。今闻和尚一说，便契本心。弟子生死事大，和尚大慈，更为教示。
Zhicheng thanked the Master and said, "I have been a disciple of Shenxiu for nine years, but without any breakthrough. Today, your words immediately made me realize the fundamental mind. For me, to transcend life and death is paramount. Most Venerable, please give me further instruction."

师曰：吾闻汝师教示学人戒定慧法，未审汝师说戒定慧行相如何？与吾说看。
The Master said, "I heard that your master also taught discipline, concentration, and wisdom. So, what exactly did he teach? Share some."

诚曰：秀大师说，诸恶莫作名为戒，诸善奉行名为慧，自净其意名为定。彼说如此，未审和尚以何法诲人？
Zhicheng replied, "Master Shenxiu said, 'To refrain from the unwholesome is discipline; to remain committed to the wholesome, wisdom; to purify the mind, concentration.' This is his instruction.

What about yours, Most Venerable?"

师曰：吾若言有法与人，即为诳汝。但且随方解缚，假名三昧。如汝师所说戒定慧，实不可思议；吾所见戒定慧又别。

The Master replied, "I would be a liar if I had claimed I could share Dharma. I only free people's minds when necessary. Such a liberated state is named Samādhi. Your master's teaching on discipline, concentration, and wisdom is indeed extraordinary. However, I have a different understanding."

志诚曰：戒定慧只合一种，如何更别？

Zhicheng said, "There is only one way to understand the three. How is it possible to understand them otherwise?"

师曰：汝师戒定慧，接大乘人；吾戒定慧，接最上乘人。悟解不同，见有迟疾。汝听吾说，与彼同否？吾所说法，不离自性；离体说法，名为相说，自性常迷。须知一切万法，皆从自性起用，是真戒定慧法。听吾偈曰：

The Master said, "Your master's teaching of the three is for the followers of the great vehicle while mine is for those of the supreme vehicle: these two groups of people have different levels of understanding. Listen to my teaching and compare it with your master's. My teaching derives [directly] from Intrinsic Nature while others' does not. Their teaching is based on the appearance because they are deluded. You should understand that everything functions through Intrinsic Nature. This is what the three is truly about. Now, listen to my poem:

心地无非自性戒，
心地无痴自性慧，
心地无乱自性定，
不增不减自金刚，
身去身来本三昧。

"A nonjudgmental mind is endowed with precepts;
An undeluded mind is endowed with wisdom;
An undisturbed mind is endowed with concentration;
[Indestructible] like the diamond, Intrinsic Nature neither increases nor decreases;
No matter how the body moves, the mind remains still."

诚闻偈悔谢，乃呈一偈：

Having heard the poem, Zhicheng apologized for his ignorance and thanked the Master with his poem:

五蕴幻身，幻何究竟？
回趣真如，法还不净。

"The body made up of five aggregates is an illusion.
How can something illusory be considered real?
Even the teaching itself on returning
To Suchness is impure."

师然之，复语诚曰：汝师戒定慧，劝小根智人；吾戒定慧，劝大根智人。若悟自性，亦不立菩提涅槃，亦不立解脱知见，无一法可得，方能建立万法。若解此意，亦名佛身，亦名菩提涅槃，亦名解脱知见。见性之人，立亦得、不立亦得，去来自由，无滞无碍，应用随作，应语随答，普见化身，不离自性，即得自在神通，游戏三昧，是名见性。

The Master agreed and further pointed out, "Your master's teaching of the trio is for those with inferior faculties and mine is for those with superior faculties. If one understands Intrinsic Nature, refrains from conceptualizing Bodhi, Nirvana, or liberating knowledge and realizes that nothing exists intrinsically, he is able to cognize everything through designation. If you understand Intrinsic Nature this way, you will find it has other names: the Buddha-body, Bodhi, Nirvana, or the liberating knowledge. Those who have realized Intrinsic Nature can accept anything, conceptualized or not conceptualized; they are totally free, unbound and unhindered; they act and speak spontaneously; they can manifest in many forms without losing Intrinsic Nature, gain freedom and super-powers, and regard Samsara as a playground. This is what realization of Intrinsic Nature involves."

志诚再启师曰：如何是不立义？

Zhicheng asked, "'Not conceptualized', what does it mean?"

师曰：自性无非、无痴、无乱，念念般若观照，常离法相，自由自在，纵横尽得，有何可立？自性自悟，顿悟顿修，亦无渐次，所以不立一切法。诸法寂灭，有何次第？志诚礼拜，愿为执侍，朝夕不懈。

The Master answered, "Intrinsic Nature is free of judgment, delusion, and disturbance; free and all-encompassing, the mind discerns and detaches itself from any form moment by moment, so there is nothing to conceptualize. Intrinsic Nature is to be understood and realized by oneself all at once with no stages involved, so conceptualization is not necessary. Since everything is in the state of non-arising and non-ceasing, stages are not necessary." Zhicheng paid respects and vowed to serve the Master wholeheartedly all the time.

僧志彻，江西人，本姓张，名行昌，少任侠。自南北分化，二宗主虽亡彼我，而徒侣竞起爱憎。时，北宗门人，自立秀师为第六祖，而忌祖师传衣为天下闻，乃嘱行昌来刺师。

Zhiche (secular name: Zhang Xingchang), a monk from Jiangxi, was brave and kind when he was young. The establishment of the southern and northern schools brought contention between disciples of the two schools, but there was no rivalry between the two founders. Disciples of the northern school, who claimed Shenxiu as the legitimate Sixth Patriarch, ordered Xingchang to assassinate Huineng, so that they could cover the truth that Huineng rather than Shenxiu had inherited the robe.

师心通，预知其事，即置金十两于座间。时夜暮，行昌入祖室，将欲加害。师舒颈就之，行昌挥刃者三，悉无所损。

However, the Master was quite aware of the plot through his psychic power and placed ten taels of gold on his chair. At that night, Xingchang sneaked into the Master's chamber to carry out the assassination. The Master exposed his neck for Xingchang to cut, but after taking three blows his neck remained intact.

师曰：正剑不邪，邪剑不正。只负汝金，不负汝命。
The Master said, "The sword won't work if used for an unjustified purpose. What I owed you [in a past life] was only gold, not life."

行昌惊仆，久而方苏，求哀悔过，即愿出家。
This greatly shocked Xingchang and he passed out. After a long time, he woke up, repented sincerely, and begged the Master to ordain him.

师遂与金，言：汝且去，恐徒众翻害于汝。汝可他日易形而来，吾当摄受。行昌禀旨宵遁，后投僧出家，具戒精进。
However, the Master handed him the gold and told him,"Go, otherwise my disciples may harm you. You can come next time in disguise for my instruction." Convinced, Xingchang fled that night. Later, he got ordained by another monk. He observed the precepts strictly and practiced Dharma diligently.

一日，忆师之言，远来礼觐。师曰：吾久念汝，汝来何晚？
One day, he recalled what the Master had told him and came all the way to pay homage. The Master recognized him and said, "I've been looking forward to seeing you again. What took you so long?"

曰：昨蒙和尚舍罪，今虽出家苦行，终难报德，其惟传法度生乎。弟子常览《涅槃经》，未晓常、无常义，乞和尚慈悲，略为解说。
He replied, “I have been so grateful for what you did back then. Currently, I am strongly committed to practice [as a way to repay your kindness], but I still feel much indebted to you. The only thing I can do for you, I guess, is to receive your teaching and spread it. Today, I came for your teaching on the *Mahāparinirvāṇa Sutra*, which I usually read. Could you please explain ‘permanent’ and ‘impermanent’ for me?”

师曰：无常者，即佛性也；有常者，即一切善恶诸法分别心也。
The Master replied, “Impermanent is Buddha Nature while permanent is the mind that conceptualizes everything, wholesome or unwholesome.”

曰：和尚所说，大违经文。
Xingchang said, “But what you said totally contradicts the Sutra.”

师曰：吾传佛心印，安敢违于佛经？
The Master replied, “I dare not teach something that contradicts the Sutra. I’ve always been teaching what Buddha taught.”

曰：经说佛性是常，和尚却言无常；善恶之法，乃至菩提心，皆是无常，和尚却言是常，此即相违，令学人转加疑惑。
Xingchang said, “Buddha Nature is permanent according to the Sutra but impermanent according to you. [According to the Sutra,]

everything conditioned including the aspiration for Buddhahood is impermanent, but you said otherwise. This glaring contradiction confuses me even more."

师曰：《涅槃经》，吾昔听尼无尽藏读诵一遍，便为讲说，无一字一义不合经文。乃至为汝，终无二说。
The Master replied, "I once heard the *Mahāparinirvāṇa Sutra* from Bhikshuni Wujinzang and expounded it for her. My words never distorted the Sutra. Likewise, what I told you just now was not against Dharma."

曰：学人识量浅昧，愿和尚委曲开示。
Xingchang said, "Sorry for my ignorance and dullness. Could you please take the trouble to explain further?"

师曰：汝知否？佛性若常，更说什么善恶诸法，乃至穷劫，无有一人发菩提心者。故吾说无常，正是佛说真常之道也。
The Master explained, "If Buddha Nature were permanent, nothing wholesome or unwholesome would exist, and nobody would ever aspire to attain Buddhahood. Thus, 'impermanent' meant by me corresponds with 'permanent' truly meant by Buddha.

又，一切诸法若无常者，即物物皆有自性，容受生死，而真常性有不遍之处。故吾说常者，正是佛说真无常义。
"If everything [manifested by the omnipresent Buddha Nature] is impermanent, it means everything has the self-nature that is subject

to life and death. This will lead to the case that Buddha Nature, the 'permanent', is not omnipresent. Thus, 'permanent' meant by me corresponds with 'impermanent' truly meant by Buddha.

佛比为凡夫外道执于邪常，诸二乘人于常计无常，共成八倒。故于涅槃了义教中，破彼偏见，而显说真常、真乐、真我、真净。汝今依言背义，以断灭无常，及确定死常，而错解佛之圆妙最后微言，纵览千遍，有何所益？

"Ordinary and heretical people are obsessed with false views on 'permanent', and sages of other vehicles mistake 'permanent' for 'impermanent'. In total, there are eight false views like these. In order to correct them, Buddha taught the 'true permanence' in *Mahāparinirvāṇa Sutra* together with the concepts of 'true happiness', 'true self', and 'true purity'. Now, your literal interpretation fails to correspond with Buddha's final teaching, a teaching that is perfect and profound. If you literally take annihilation for 'impermanent' and take absolute stillness for true 'permanent', you will gain no benefit no matter how many times you read the Sutra."

行昌忽然大悟，说偈云：

Inspired by his sudden insight, Xingchang came up with a poem:

因守无常心，佛说有常性；
不知方便者，犹春池拾砾。
我今不施功，佛性而现前；
非师相授与，我亦无所得。

"To rid people of their attachment to impermanence,
Buddha taught permanence of Intrinsic Nature.
If you miss the point [of such skillful teaching],
You are like a person who is oblivious to the scenic pond
—what you came for—
And distracted by the pebbles.
Now without deliberate cultivation,
Buddha Nature manifests itself.
You have nothing to give,
And I have nothing to take."

师曰：汝今彻也，宜名志彻。彻礼谢而退。

The Master replied, "Now you get it completely, so you shall be called Zhiche, which means full enlightenment." Zhiche thanked the Master and left.

有一童子，名神会，襄阳高氏子，年十三，自玉泉来参礼。

Shenhui, a thirteen-year-old boy of Gao family in Xiangyang, came from Yuquan Temple to pay homage.

师曰：知识远来艰辛，还将得本来否？若有本则合识主，试说看。

The Master asked, "My Dharma friend, it must have been a long and tough journey for you. I wonder if you have realized Intrinsic Nature. If so, you must have already met the real host [of your mind and body]. Please share your understanding!"

会曰：以无住为本，见即是主。

Shenhui answered, “The host is the seeing mind that originally dwells on nothing.”

师曰：这沙弥争合取次语！

The Master replied, “You sure talk big!”

会乃问曰：和尚坐禅，还见不见？

Shenhui asked, “Most Venerable, in your meditation, you see anything or not?”

师以柱杖打三下，云：吾打汝痛不痛？对曰：亦痛亦不痛。

The Master struck him with the staff three times and asked, “You feel the pain or not?” And he replied, “Neither.”

师曰：吾亦见亦不见。

The Master said, “My answer to your question is likewise: neither.”

神会问：如何是亦见亦不见？

Shenhui asked, “How come?”

师云：吾之所见，常见自心过愆，不见他人是非好恶，是以亦见亦不见。汝言亦痛亦不痛如何？汝若不痛，同其木石；若痛，则同凡夫，即起恚恨。汝向前见不见是二边，痛不痛是生灭。汝自性且不见，敢尔弄人！

The Master explained, “I see my own faults and don’t see others’.

How can you feel the pain and don't feel it at the same time? If you don't feel the pain, you are no different from trees and rocks. If you do, you are no different from ordinary beings, who are easily disturbed by anger and hatred. Your question whether I see anything or not in my meditation is the very proof that you are bound by a dualistic view. The claim that you feel the pain and don't feel it at the same time indicates that you have not transcended arising and ceasing. You haven't even realized Intrinsic Nature. How dare you show off!"

神会礼拜悔谢。
Shenhui sincerely apologized for his ignorance.

师又曰：汝若心迷不见，问善知识觅路；汝若心悟，即自见性，依法修行。汝自迷不见自心，却来问吾见与不见。吾见自知，岂代汝迷？汝若自见，亦不代吾迷。何不自知自见，乃问吾见与不见？
The Master continued, "Seek guidance from a spiritual teacher if you are deluded, which means you haven't realized Intrinsic Nature. Practice according to Dharma if you are awakened, which means you have realized Intrinsic Nature. Without having realized Intrinsic Nature, how could you come to ask me if I see anything or not? My realization, which is only accessible to myself, can hardly help you dispel your delusion. Likewise, your realization would be of no use to me. Therefore, you should realize Intrinsic Nature by yourself and stop asking me if I see anything or not."

神会再礼百余拜，求谢过愆，服勤给侍，不离左右。

[Out of shame,] Shenhui bowed repeatedly to the Master. Since then, he dedicated himself to serving the Master.

一日，师告众曰：吾有一物，无头无尾，无名无字，无背无面，诸人还识否？

One day, the Master told the assembly, "I have something that has no name, no head and tail, no back and front. Do you know what it is?"

神会出曰：是诸佛之本源，神会之佛性。

Shenhui came forward and replied, "It is the origin of buddhas and also my Buddha Nature."

师曰：向汝道无名无字，汝便唤作本源佛性。汝向去有把茆盖头，也只成个知解宗徒。

The Master replied in disapproval, "As I said, it has no name, yet you call it the origin and Buddha Nature. Even though regarded as an eminent monk in the future, you will only be able to understand and interpret my teachings theoretically."

祖师灭后，会入京洛，大弘曹溪顿教，著《显宗记》，盛行于世，是为荷泽禅师。

After the Master's demise, Shenhui went to Luoyang and spread Sudden Teaching there. He was famous for his *Xian Zong Ji* (An Explicit Treatise on Chan Teaching) and later known as the Chan Master of Heze School.

师见诸宗难问，咸起恶心，多集座下，愍而谓曰：学道之人，一切善念恶念，应当尽除。无名可名，名于自性；无二之性，是名实性。于实性上建立一切教门，言下便须自见。

The Master was often met with challenges by hostile followers of other schools, so he gathered them and addressed them with compassion:"As Dharma learners, you should get rid of all thoughts, either wholesome or unwholesome, [and realize] what is expediently called Intrinsic Nature, which is beyond names. It is also called the 'true nature', though it is not different from anything else by essence. Teachings established on the true nature will lead the learners to Intrinsic Nature at once."

诸人闻说，总皆作礼，请事为师。

After hearing these words, they all thanked the Master and were willing to learn from him.

护法品第九
Chapter 9
Dharma-protection

神龙元年上元日，则天中宗诏云：朕请安秀二师，宫中供养。万机之暇，每究一乘。二师推让云：南方有能禅师，密受忍大师衣法，传佛心印，可请彼问。今遣内侍薛简，驰诏请迎，愿师慈念，速赴上京。

On the first full-moon day in 705 C.E., Her Majesty Wu Zetian and Emperor Li Xian, her son, sent a royal decree to the Master, which said, "To make time for the knowledge of the supreme vehicle, we invited Master Hui'an and Master Shenxiu to stay in the royal palace, but they would always redirect us to Master Huineng in the south, the recipient of Master Hongren's robe and the disseminator of Buddha's authentic teaching. That's why we order Xue Jian, the royal attendant to invite your Most Venerable to the capital. We wish your Most Venerable could kindly accept the invitation and set off at your earliest convenience!"

师上表辞疾，愿终林麓。薛简曰：京城禅德皆云，欲得会道，必须坐禅习定；若不因禅定而得解脱者，未之有也。未审师所说法如何？

The Master declined the offer with the excuse of his sickness and expressed his wish to spend the rest of his life in the mountain. Xue Jian asked the Master, "Renowned Chan masters in the capital all asserted that absorption through sitting meditation is the only path to spiritual achievement, and that nobody has ever attained liberation otherwise. May I know your opinion?"

师曰：道由心悟，岂在坐也？经云：若言如来若坐若卧，是行邪道。何故？无所从来，亦无所去。无生无灭，是如来清净禅。诸法空寂，是如来清净坐。究竟无证，岂况坐耶？

The Master replied, "Spiritual attainment depends on the awakening of the mind, so don't cling to sitting. According to the *Diamond Sutra*, 'If anyone holds that Tathāgata (Thus-gone, namely Buddha) sits, lies down, and so on, this person is following a wrong path. Why? Because Tathāgata neither comes nor goes.' Without arising and ceasing, everything being intrinsically empty and still, this is the state of Tathāgata. This ultimate reality is not to be realized through practice at all, let alone sitting."

简曰：弟子回京，主上必问。愿师慈悲，指示心要，传奏两宫，及京城学道者。譬如一灯燃百千灯，冥者皆明，明明无尽。

Jian said, "The royal family will definitely ask about your teaching when I return. Please kindly share with me the essence of your teaching so that I can report to the royal family and other Dharma learners in the capital. One lamp can light up thousands of other lamps, dispelling darkness with boundless light."

师云：道无明暗，明暗是代谢之义。明明无尽，亦是有尽，相待立名。故《净名经》云：法无有比，无相待故。

The Master replied, "Light and darkness take turns to appear while Dharma transcends both. By saying boundless light, you have already presumed there are bounds. 'Boundless' and 'bound' are nothing but dualistic concepts. As the *Vimalakīrti Sutra* says, 'Dharma is beyond duality and cannot be completely explained through metaphors.'"

简曰：明喻智慧，暗喻烦恼。修道之人，倘不以智慧照破烦恼，无始生死，凭何出离？

Jian went on with his inquiry, "The light is like wisdom; the darkness, defilements. If a practitioner does not dispel the darkness of defilements with the light of wisdom, how can he put an end to the cycle of birth-and-death?"

师曰：烦恼即是菩提，无二无别。若以智慧照破烦恼者，此是二乘见解。羊鹿等机，上智大根，悉不如是。

The Master answered, "Defilements and Bodhi (awakening) share the same essence; they are not different. Only learners of lesser faculties would hold that discernment of wisdom dispels defilements, a view with which Mahayana practitioners of superior faculties would disagree."

简曰：如何是大乘见解？
Jian asked, “Tell me more about the view of Mahayana.”

师曰：明与无明，凡夫见二。智者了达，其性无二。无二之性，即是实性。实性者，处凡愚而不减，在贤圣而不增，住烦恼而不乱，居禅定而不寂。不断不常，不来不去，不在中间，及其内外。不生不灭，性相如如。常住不迁，名之曰道。
The Master said, “Light of wisdom and darkness of ignorance are distinctively two things to the ordinary beings, but the same thing (Intrinsic Nature) to the sages. Intrinsic Nature remains as it is in any state: delusion will not decrease it; wisdom will not increase it; defilements will not disturb it, and concentration will not still it. It does not cease to be, nor does it last forever. It does not come, nor does it go. It is not outside, inside, or in between. It does not arise, nor does it cease to be. Its nature and characters are just as such. It is beyond change and expediently named Suchness.”

简曰：师说不生不灭，何异外道？
Jian asked, “When you say it neither arises nor ceases, are you talking about the same thing as the heretics talk about?”

师曰：外道所说不生不灭者，将灭止生，以生显灭，灭犹不灭，生说不生。我说不生不灭者，本自无生，今亦不灭，所以不同外道。汝若欲知心要，但一切善恶，都莫思量，自然得入清净心体。湛然常寂，妙用恒沙。
The Master replied, “When they talk about it, they mean that arising is

the antithesis of cessation: the existence of one excludes the other. In such a dualistic view, so-called cessation is not the ultimate cessation, and so-called arising is not permanent. When I talk about it, I mean the ultimate, which does not arise in the first place and hence no cessation. To get the essence of my teaching, your mind shall neither dwell on the wholesome nor the unwholesome. By doing so, the pure essence of the mind—eternally clear and peaceful, manifesting itself through functions as numerous as the sand grains of the Ganges—will be unveiled."

简蒙指教，豁然大悟，礼辞归阙，表奏师语。

Greatly inspired by the teaching, Jian bid farewell to the Master and went back to report what he had learned.

其年九月三日，有诏奖谕师曰：师辞老疾，为朕修道，国之福田。师若净名，托疾毗耶，阐扬大乘，传诸佛心，谈不二法。薛简传师指授如来知见。朕积善余庆，宿种善根。值师出世，顿悟上乘。感荷师恩，顶戴无已，并奉磨衲袈裟，及水晶钵，敕韶州刺史，修饰寺宇，赐师旧居，为国恩寺。

In the same year, on the third day of the ninth lunar month, the emperor issued another decree to extoll and reward the Master, which read, "Due to advanced age and poor health, Your Most Venerable declined my previous invitation, but your dedication to Dharma has benefited me. You are indeed the field of merit for this country. What you did is exactly what Vimalakirti did: by using his sickness as an excuse, he stayed in Vaishali, spreading the Mahayana teaching (the essence of

Buddha Nature and non-duality). Xue Jian shared your teaching on the Buddha's knowledge with me, and I immediately understood this teaching on the supreme vehicle. This must be the result of the merit that I accumulated in the past lives which allowed us to live in the same time. Therefore, you deserve my deepest gratitude and reverence. As a token of such, please kindly accept this special robe and the crystal bowl. We order the governor in Shaozhou to renovate your temple. In addition, we will convert your residence while you were a lay person into 'Guo'en (royal grace) Temple'."

付嘱品第十
Chapter 10
Final Instructions

师一日唤门人法海、志诚、法达、神会、智常、智通、志彻、志道、法珍、法如等，曰：汝等不同余人，吾灭度后，各为一方师。吾今教汝说法，不失本宗。先须举三科法门，动用三十六对，出没即离两边，说一切法，莫离自性。忽有人问汝法，出语尽双，皆取对法，来去相因。究竟二法尽除，更无去处。

One day, the Master summoned his disciples Fahai, Zhicheng, Fada, Shenhui, Zhichang, Zhitong, Zhiche, Zhidao, Fazhen, and Faru, and told them, "You are distinguished from others, and each of you shall carry on my teaching in different places after my death. Now I am telling you how to do it correctly. Start with Three Classifications; employ Thirty-six Pairs [of antithetical concepts] to avoid clinging to either pole in a pair; never deviate from Intrinsic Nature whenever you teach. Whenever you have to answer a question, bring up a pair of concepts that are antithetical and mutually dependent. When the inquirer is denied to either pole, he will be cornered and have no foothold.

三科法门者，阴界入也。阴是五阴：色受想行识是也。入是十二入，外六尘：色声香味触法；内六门：眼耳鼻舌身意是也。界是十八界：六尘、六门、六识是也。自性能含万法，名含藏识。若起思量，即是转识。生六识，出六门，见六尘，如是一十八界，皆从自性起用。自性若邪，起十八邪；自性若正，起十八正。若恶用即众生用，善用即佛用。用由何等，由自性有。

"The Three Classifications are the aggregates (skandha), elements (dhātu), and sense bases (āyatana). The Five Aggregates are matter, feelings, perception, mental formations, and consciousness. The Twelve Bases are the six external objects (visible form, sound, odor, taste, tangible object, and mental object) and the six internal faculties① (eyes, ears, nose, tongue, body, and mind). The Eighteen Elements are the six objects, the six faculties, and the six consciousnesses②. Intrinsic Nature is all-encompassing, hence the name the "store-consciousness". From this consciousness, the functioning consciousness arises when there is a cognizing process, and the first six consciousnesses arise to cognize the six objects through the six faculties. In this way, the eighteen elements function through Intrinsic Nature. When Intrinsic Nature is veiled by defilements, these eighteen elements will be defiled; when it is free from defilements, the eighteen elements will be undefiled. When Intrinsic Nature gives rise to unwholesome functions, this is the state of ordinary beings. When it gives rise to wholesome

① The six internal faculties: Six Gates.

② The six consciousnesses: Five sensory consciousnesses including visual, auditory, olfactory, gustatory, and tactile consciousnesses, plus mind consciousness.

functions, this is the state of Buddha. Where are these functions from? From Intrinsic Nature.

对法：外境无情五对：天与地对，日与月对，明与暗对，阴与阳对，水与火对，此是五对也。

“There are five pairs of non-sentient external objects: the heaven and the earth, the sun and the moon, light and darkness, *yin* and *yang*, water and fire.

法相语言十二对：语与法对，有与无对，有色与无色对，有相与无相对，有漏与无漏对，色与空对，动与静对，清与浊对，凡与圣对，僧与俗对，老与少对，大与小对，此是十二对也。

“There are twelve pairs of characteristics and names: the name and the object, the existent and the nonexistent, the material and the immaterial, the forms and the formless, the defiled and the undefiled, the corporeality and the emptiness, the dynamic and the static, the clear and the cloudy, the mundane and the supramundane, the monastics and the laity, the old and the young, the large and the small.

自性起用十九对：长与短对，邪与正对，痴与慧对，愚与智对，乱与定对，慈与毒对，戒与非对，直与曲对，实与虚对，险与平对，烦恼与菩提对，常与无常对，悲与害对，喜与瞋对，舍与悭对，进与退对，生与灭对，法身与色身对，化身与报身对，此是十九对也。

“There are nineteen pairs that arise through Intrinsic Nature: length and shortness, falsehood and correctness, ignorance and wisdom, foolishness and intelligence, distraction and concentration, loving-kindness and cruelty, morality and immorality, integrity and crookedness, substance and non-substance, unevenness and evenness, defilements and Bodhi, permanence and impermanence, compassion and malice, joy and anger, generosity and stinginess, progression and regression, arising and ceasing, the Dharma-body and the physical body, the Manifestation-body and the Enjoyment-body."

师言：此三十六对法，若解用，即道贯一切经法，出入即离两边。自性动用，共人言语，外于相离相，内于空离空。

The Master said, "If you know how to employ these Thirty-Six Pairs, you will be able to expound doctrines without clinging to either pole. When you converse with people, discern the functioning Intrinsic Nature so that you can be detached from what you experience: forms and emptiness.

若全着相，即长邪见。若全执空，即长无明。执空之人有谤经，直言不用文字。既云不用文字，人亦不合语言。只此语言，便是文字之相。又云直道不立文字，即此不立两字，亦是文字。见人所说，便即谤他言着文字。汝等须知，自迷犹可，又谤佛经。不要谤经，罪障无数。

"Attachment to forms leads to wrong views; attachment to emptiness leads to ignorance. Those attached to nothingness do a great disservice to the sutras by saying that words are unnecessary. If words were unnecessary, people should not speak at all because speech itself is made of words. They also claim that the direct path does not rely on words, yet this claim is made possible by words. They will criticize whoever uses language for clinging to words. You should know that they are being deluded and doing a disservice to scriptures, which is something one should never do because it will cause great unwholesome karma.

若着相于外，而作法求真，或广立道场，说有无之过患，如是之人，累劫不得见性。但听依法修行，又莫百物不思，而于道性窒碍。若听说不修，令人反生邪念。但依法修行，无住相法施。汝等若悟，依此说，依此用，依此行，依此作，即不失本宗。

"If you seek externally for the truth by performing rituals or engage in criticism of either existence or nonexistence when spreading Dharma, you will not realize Intrinsic Nature even for eons. You should practice according to Dharma. Never suppress your thoughts, otherwise your practice will be hindered. Listening to Dharma without practicing it, you will be led astray. Just follow Dharma and spread it without a clinging mind. If you get it, you should teach, practice, behave and act accordingly. In this way, the spirit of our teaching won't be lost.

若有人问汝义，问有，将无对；问无，将有对；问凡，以圣对；问圣，以凡对。二道相因，生中道义。如一问一对，余问一依此作，即不失理也。

"When asked about existence, you should talk about nonexistence; when asked about nonexistence, you should talk about existence. When asked about the mundane, you should talk about the supramundane; when asked about the supramundane, you should talk about the mundane. Pairs of mutually dependent and antithetical concepts point to the middle way, so employ them in your teaching. By doing so, you won't deviate from the truth.

设有人问：何名为暗？答云：明是因，暗是缘，明没则暗，以明显暗，以暗显明，来去相因，成中道义。余问悉皆如此。汝等于后传法，依此转相教授，勿失宗旨。

"If someone asks what darkness is, you can tell him that light and darkness condition and define each other: when one is absent, the other is present. The fact that they are mutually dependent reveals the middle way. Deal with all other questions in this way and pass on this approach so that the spirit of our teaching won't be lost."

师于太极元年壬子，延和七月，命门人，往新州国恩寺建塔。仍令促工。次年夏末落成。七月一日，集徒众曰：吾至八月，欲离世间。汝等有疑，早须相问，为汝破疑，令汝迷尽。吾若去后，无人教汝。法海等闻，悉皆涕泣。惟有神会，神情不动，亦无涕泣。

In the seventh lunar month of year 712 C.E., the Master ordered his disciples to build a stupa for him at Guo'en Temple in Xinzhou and pressed for a quick completion. The construction was completed at the end of next summer. On the first day of the seventh lunar month, the Master summoned all his disciples and announced, "I will leave this world next month. If you have any doubts, ask me now so that I can clear them up and remove all your delusions. After my death, nobody will teach you anymore." Hearing this, Fahai and others all cried except Shenhui, who was calm without tears.

师云：神会小师，却得善不善等，毁誉不动，哀乐不生，余者不得。数年山中，竟修何道？汝今悲泣，为忧阿谁？若忧吾不知去处，吾自知去处。吾若不知去处，终不预报于汝。汝等悲泣，盖为不知吾去处。若知吾去处，即不合悲泣。

The Master said, "Young as Venerable Shenhui is, he has achieved such a state in which he treats good and bad equally without being moved by praise or blame, joy or sorrow. The rest of you, however, have not achieved this state. What on earth have you been practicing all these years in the mountain? Who are you shedding tears for? If you are shedding tears for me, it's unnecessary because I clearly know where I will go after my death. Otherwise, I wouldn't have informed you in advance. Perhaps, it is because you don't know where I will go. If you knew, you wouldn't cry.

法性本无生灭去来，汝等尽坐，吾与汝说一偈，名曰：真假动静偈。汝等诵取此偈，与吾意同，依此修行，不失宗旨。

"Intrinsic Nature does not arise and cease, nor does it come and go in the first place. Please sit down and listen to my poem entitled *On Truth and Illusion, Motion and Stillness*. Chant and apply it so that you can fully understand me; follow its instructions so that you will not misinterpret the teaching."

众僧作礼，请师作偈，偈曰：

Bowing to the Master, the monks requested for the poem, which went:

一切无有真，不以见于真，
若见于真者，是见尽非真。
若能自有真，离假即心真，
自心不离假，无真何处真？
有情即解动，无情即不动，
若修不动行，同无情不动。
若觅真不动，动上有不动，
不动是不动，无情无佛种。

"Things are unreal.
Don't take what you cognize as real.
The view that what you cognize is real
Is not true.
Once Intrinsic Nature is realized,
The unreal will be replaced with the Truth.
If your mind is attached to the unreal,
How can the Truth manifest itself?
Sentient beings can move,
While non-sentient beings cannot.
If a practitioner tries to stay motionless,
He is nothing more than a non-sentient being.
If you really want to seek what is ultimately motionless,
You'd better focus on that which is beyond motions.
Conventionally, whatever is motionless
Has neither Buddha-seed nor sentience.

能善分别相，第一义不动，
但作如是见，即是真如用。
报诸学道人，努力须用意，
莫于大乘门，却执生死智。
若言下相应，即共论佛义，
若实不相应，合掌令欢喜。
此宗本无诤，诤即失道意，
执逆诤法门，自性入生死。

"Cognize everything skillfully
With Intrinsic Nature undisturbed.
By doing so, the function of Suchness
Can manifest itself.
Dharma pursuers, listen to me,
You must practice diligently.
Since you are learning Mahayana,
Do not cling to the knowledge of life and death.
If what you say resonates with someone,
Discuss doctrines with him then.
If there is no resonance,
Stop the conversation and join your palms instead.
Our teaching involves no argument;
Once you argue, you forget the purpose of Dharma.
If you insist on the superiority of a particular teaching,
Intrinsic Nature will be clouded, and you'll end up in Samsara."

时徒众闻说偈已，普皆作礼。并体师意，各各摄心，依法修行，更不敢诤。

After hearing this poem, all the disciples thanked the Master sincerely. Having understood what the Master said, they were pacified and ready for the practice as instructed, thus no more argument among them.

乃知大师不久住世。法海上座，再拜问曰：和尚入灭之后，衣法当付何人？

Everyone knew that the Master would pass away soon. Then, Elder Fahai came to pay homage to the Master and asked, "Most Venerable, who shall inherit your robe and teaching after you pass away?"

师曰：吾于大梵寺说法，以至于今，抄录流行，目曰：《法宝坛经》。汝等守护，递相传授，度诸群生。但依此说，是名正法。今为汝等说法，不付其衣。盖为汝等信根淳熟，决定无疑，堪任大事。然据先祖达摩大师，付授偈意，衣不合传。偈曰：

The Master replied, "Record what I have been teaching at Dafan Temple and compile it into a book entitled *The Dharma Jewel Platform Sutra* for circulation. All of you must preserve and pass it on to liberate sentient beings. Just follow the teaching in it, which is the authentic Dharma. Now I'll pass on the teaching, not the robe. For one thing, you are surely qualified to hold the lineage as you have unshakable faith in my teaching. For another, as instructed by Bodhidharma the First Patriarch in his poem, there is no need to pass on the robe. The poem reads:

吾本来兹土，传法救迷情。
一花开五叶，结果自然成。

"I came to this land with a mission of spreading Dharma
To liberate the deluded sentient beings.
Like a bud that bursts into a flower with five petals,
My teaching will branch into five
that will eventually establish themselves."

师复曰：诸善知识，汝等各各净心，听吾说法。若欲成就种智，须达一相三昧，一行三昧。若于一切处而不住相，于彼相中不生憎爱，亦无取舍，不念利益成坏等事，安闲恬静，虚融澹泊，此名一相三昧。若于一切处，行住坐卧，纯一直心，不动道场，真成净土，此名一行三昧。若人具二三昧，如地有种，含藏长养，成熟其实，一相一行，亦复如是。我今说法，犹如时雨，普润大地。汝等佛性，譬诸种子，遇兹沾洽，悉皆发生。承吾旨者，决获菩提；依吾行者，定证妙果。听吾偈曰：

The Master went on, "My Dharma friends, now clear your mind and listen to my teaching. Through One-form Samādhi and One-practice Samādhi, you can attain All-encompassing Wisdom. One-form Samādhi refers to the state in which one's mind does not cling to any form at any time. In this state, free from hatred and love, and a sense of gain and loss, he remains collected, desireless, peaceful, and receptive. One-practice Samādhi refers to the state in which one's mind is authentic and undisturbed under any circumstance: walking, standing, sitting, or lying. This state is where Pure Land exactly is. These two Samādhi-s, once attained can bring benefits as soil enables seeds to grow and yield fruits. This teaching is like timely rain that nourishes beings on the earth. Your Buddha Nature is like the seeds that wake up in the rain. Those who practice according to my instruction will definitely obtain Bodhi, the spiritual fruit. Listen to this poem of mine:

心地含诸种，普雨悉皆萌。
顿悟华情已，菩提果自成。
"Seeds in the field of mind
Sprout in the rain,
And the flower of awakening
Turns into the fruit of Bodhi naturally."

师说偈已，曰：其法无二，其心亦然。其道清净，亦无诸相。汝等慎勿观静，及空其心；此心本净，无可取舍，各自努力，随缘好去。尔时，徒众作礼而退。

Then, the Master continued, "Dharma and the mind are beyond duality, and there are neither defilements nor forms in the Path. Be careful not to cling to stillness and emptiness, because the mind, in which there is nothing to grasp or reject, is pure in the first place. Each of you, practice hard from now on under any circumstance." Then, all the disciples thanked him and left.

大师七月八日，忽谓门人曰：吾欲归新州，汝等速理舟楫。大众哀留甚坚。

On the eighth day of the seventh lunar month, the Master suddenly told his disciples, "I want to return to Xinzhou, my hometown. Prepare a boat for me quickly." However, they sincerely begged him to stay.

师曰：诸佛出现，犹示涅槃。有来必去，理亦常然。吾此形骸，归必有所。

The Master said, "Even buddhas take their departure after their mission in this world. It's quite natural that whatever comes must go. This body of mine has to return to its place of birth."

众曰：师从此去，早晚可回。

The disciples asked, "Master, but when will you come back?"

师曰：叶落归根，来时无口。

The Master replied, "As fallen leaves find their resting place under the tree, [I will also return to my birthplace]. Even though I would come back, I wouldn't have anything to teach."

又问曰：正法眼藏，传付何人？

Then they asked, "Who will carry on your teaching?"

师曰：有道者得，无心者通。

The Master answered, "Those with attainment and non-attaching mind."

又问：后莫有难否？

They asked further, "Should we brace ourselves for anything?"

师曰：吾灭后五六年，当有一人来取吾首。听吾记曰：
The Master answered, “Five or six years after my death, someone will come to steal my head. Listen to my prophecy:

头上养亲，口里须餐。
遇满之难，杨柳为官。

“Paid by someone who wants to worship my head,
An impoverished man called Man will come to steal it
At the time when Yang and Liu govern here.”

又云: 吾去七十年，有二菩萨，从东方来，一出家、一在家。同时兴化，建立吾宗，缔缉伽蓝，昌隆法嗣。
He added, “Seventy years after my death, two Bodhisattvas (a monastic member and a lay person) will come from the east. Both will popularize the teaching of our school, build temples and make our lineage thrive.”

问曰：未知从上佛祖应现已来，传授几代，愿垂开示。
They inquired, “Since the teaching was first revealed, how many times has it been passed on so far? Could you please tell us?”

师云：古佛应世，已无数量，不可计也。今以七佛为始。过去庄严劫毗婆尸佛，尸弃佛，毗舍浮佛；今贤劫拘留孙佛，拘那含牟尼佛，迦叶佛，释迦文佛，是为七佛。
The Master answered, “Countless times by innumerable buddhas. I will list the latest seven. They are Vipashyin Buddha, Shikhin Buddha,

and Vishvabhu Buddha of the Adorned Eon; Krakucchanda Buddha, Kanakamuni Buddha, Kashyapa Buddha, and Shakyamuni Buddha of the Distinguished Eon.

释迦文佛首传摩诃迦叶尊者，第二阿难尊者，第三商那和修尊者，第四优波毱多尊者，第五提多迦尊者，第六弥遮迦尊者，第七婆须蜜多尊者，第八佛驮难提尊者，第九伏驮蜜多尊者，第十胁尊者，第十一富那夜奢尊者，第十二马鸣大士，第十三迦毗摩罗尊者，第十四龙树大士，第十五迦那提婆尊者，第十六罗睺罗多尊者，第十七僧伽难提尊者，第十八伽耶舍多尊者，第十九鸠摩罗多尊者，第二十阇耶多尊者，第二十一婆修盘头尊者，第二十二摩拏罗尊者，第二十三鹤勒那尊者，第二十四师子尊者，第二十五婆舍斯多尊者，第二十六不如蜜多尊者，第二十七般若多罗尊者，第二十八菩提达摩尊者，第二十九慧可大师，第三十僧璨大师，第三十一道信大师，第三十二弘忍大师，惠能是为三十三祖。从上诸祖，各有禀承，汝等向后，递代流传，毋令乖误。

"From Shakyamuni Buddha onwards, it has been passed to Arya Mahakasyapa, the First Patriarch; Arya Ananda, the Second; Arya Sanavasa, the Third; Arya Upagupta, the Fourth; Arya Dhrtaka, the Fifth; Arya Micchaka, the Sixth; Arya Vasumitra, the Seventh; Arya Buddhanandi, the Eighth; Arya Punyamitra, the Ninth; Arya Parshva, the Tenth; Arya Punyayasas, the Eleventh; Arya Asvaghosa, the Twelfth; Arya Kapimala, the Thirteenth; Mahasattva Nagarjuna, the Fourteenth; Arya Kanadeva, the Fifteenth; Arya Rahulata, the Sixteenth; Arya Sanghanandi, the Seventeenth; Arya Jayashata, the Eighteenth; Arya Kumarata, the Nineteenth; Arya Jayata, the

Twentieth; Arya Vasubandhu, the Twenty-first; Arya Manora, the Twenty-second; Arya Haklena, the Twenty-third; Arya Sinha, the Twenty-fourth; Arya Vasasita, the Twenty-fifth; Arya Punyamitra, the Twenty-sixth; Arya Prajnatara, the Twenty-seventh; Arya Bodhidharma, the Twenty-eighth; Master Huike, the Twenty-ninth; Master Sengcan, the Thirtieth; Master Daoxin, the Thirty-first; Master Hongren, the Thirty-second; and me, Huineng, the Thirty-third. The teaching has been carried on from one generation to another. You shall also pass on the teaching without altering it."

大师先天二年癸丑岁，八月初三日，于国恩寺斋罢，谓诸徒众曰：汝等各依位坐，吾与汝别。

On the third day of the eighth lunar month, year 713 C.E., after his meal at Guo'en Temple, the Master told his disciples, "Each of you, please take your seat. Now I have to say farewell."

法海白言：和尚留何教法，令后代迷人，得见佛性？

Fahai asked, "Most Venerable, could you please give some instructions on how to realize Buddha Nature to the deluded in future?"

师言：汝等谛听，后代迷人，若识众生，即是佛性；若不识众生，万劫觅佛难逢。吾今教汝识自心众生，见自心佛性。欲求见佛，但识众生；只为众生迷佛，非是佛迷众生。自性若悟，众生是佛；自性若迷，佛是众生。自性平等，众生是佛；自性邪险，佛是众生。汝等心若险曲，即佛在众生中；一念平直，即是众生成佛。我心自有佛，自佛是真佛。自若无佛心，何处求真佛？汝等自心是佛，更莫狐疑。外无一物而能建立，皆是本心生万种法。故经云：心生种种法生，心灭种种法灭。吾今留一偈，与汝等别，名自性真佛偈。后代之人，识此偈意，自见本心，自成佛道。偈曰：

The Master said, "Listen to me carefully. If the deluded in future recognize the nature of sentient beings, they can know Buddha Nature; if not, they won't be able to see Buddha even for eons. Recognize in your mind sentient beings and Buddha Nature. Recognize sentient beings, and you will see Buddha. The truth is that sentient beings don't know they themselves are buddhas, but buddhas know that well. With realized Intrinsic Nature, sentient beings are buddhas; with unrealized Intrinsic Nature, buddhas are sentient beings. When Intrinsic Nature functions in a nonjudgmental way, sentient beings are buddhas; when Intrinsic Nature functions in a distorted way, buddhas are sentient beings. The moment the mind is distorted, buddhas will be in the state of sentient beings; the moment the mind is undefiled, sentient beings will be in the state of buddha. The buddha within is the real buddha. If you fail to see the mind as a buddha, where else can you find the real one? Your very mind is the buddha! Never doubt it! Ultimately, there is nothing out there. Things are merely the manifestations of the original mind. As the sutra says, 'When the mind arises, things come into being; when the mind ceases, things cease to be.' Now I give you a farewell poem entitled *Intrinsic Nature: the Real Buddha*. If people in future understand the poem, they will see their original mind and attain Buddhahood eventually. The poem goes:

真如自性是真佛，邪见三毒是魔王，
邪迷之时魔在舍，正见之时佛在堂。
性中邪见三毒生，即是魔王来住舍，
正见自除三毒心，魔变成佛真无假。
法身报身及化身，三身本来是一身，
若向性中能自见，即是成佛菩提因。

"Suchness (Intrinsic Nature) is the real buddha
While false views and Three Poisons turn into Mara (the lord of demons).
With delusion, the mind invites Mara;
With right views, it enshrines buddha.
When false views and Three Poisons arise,
Mara comes to live in the mind.
When the right views replace Three Poisons in the mind,
Mara turns into the real buddha.
Dharma-body, Enjoyment-body, and Manifestation-body
Are one in the first place.
Your realization of Intrinsic Nature
Is the cause of Bodhi (the attainment of Buddhahood).

本从化身生净性，净性常在化身中，
性使化身行正道，当来圆满真无穷。
淫性本是净性因，除淫即是净性身，
性中各自离五欲，见性刹那即是真。
今生若遇顿教门，忽悟自性见世尊，
若欲修行觅作佛，不知何处拟求真。

若能心中自见真，有真即是成佛因，
不见自性外觅佛，起心总是大痴人。
顿教法门今已留，救度世人须自修，
报汝当来学道者，不作此见大悠悠。

"Originally, the pure nature arises from the Manifestation-body,
And it is ever-present within the Manifestation-body.
This nature keeps the Manifestation-body on the right path
Until the perfection is attained.
The nature of lust is the pure nature,
Which can be unveiled once lust is removed.
Everyone's Intrinsic Nature is free of desires.
The moment it is realized, the reality manifests itself.
If you hear this teaching of Sudden Enlightenment,
You can realize Intrinsic Nature and see buddhas at once.
If you practice in order to see buddhas outside,
It means you are ignorant of where they are.
If you can find the real one within,
It can lead you to Buddhahood.
Those who are unaware of Intrinsic Nature
And believe they can find buddhas elsewhere are completely ignorant.
The teaching of Sudden Enlightenment has been given.
Follow it before you teach others.
Future learners without this view
Will waste time in their practice."

师说偈已，告曰：汝等好住，吾灭度后，莫作世情悲泣雨泪，受人吊问。身着孝服，非吾弟子，亦非正法。但识自本心，见自本性，无动无静，无生无灭，无去无来，无是无非，无住无往。恐汝等心迷，不会吾意，今再嘱汝，令汝见性。吾灭度后，依此修行，如吾在日；若违吾教，纵吾在世，亦无有益。复说偈曰：

After giving the poem, the Master said, "Please take care of yourselves. When I pass away, spare your tears, condolences, and mourning gowns. If you follow the secular way of mourning, you are neither my disciples nor followers of authentic Dharma. Try to realize your original mind (Intrinsic Nature), which neither moves nor stays still, neither arises nor ceases, neither comes nor goes, neither accepts nor denies, and neither stays nor leaves. I'm afraid that your delusion may prevent you from understanding my words, so I urge you again to realize Intrinsic Nature. After my death, if you follow the teaching, you would have me by your side; otherwise, you would receive no benefit even though I am alive." Then, the Master gave another poem:

兀兀不修善，腾腾不造恶。
寂寂断见闻，荡荡心无著。

"In peace, the mind does not produce the wholesome.
In action, it does not produce the unwholesome.
The mind is silent and untainted by what is seen or heard.
The mind is boundless and free from attachments."

师说偈已，端坐至三更，忽谓门人曰：吾行矣。奄然迁化，于时异香满室，白虹属地，林木变白，禽兽哀鸣。

After giving the poem, the Master meditated until midnight. Suddenly, he told his disciples, “I’m leaving!” Shortly, he passed away. The room was filled with extraordinary fragrance; a halo appeared, covering the ground and turning the woods white; birds and beasts cried out in sorrow.

十一月，广韶新三郡官僚，洎门人僧俗，争迎真身，莫决所之。乃焚香祷曰：香烟指处，师所归焉。时，香烟直贯曹溪。十一月十三日，迁神龛并所传衣钵而回。次年七月二十五日出龛，弟子方辩，以香泥上之。

In the eleventh lunar month, the officials and the Masters’ disciples (both the monastic members and the laypeople) from Guangzhou, Shaozhou, and Xinzhou, had a dispute over who should have the Master’s full-body relic. Since no agreement had been reached, they burnt incense and prayed, “Master, where your body shall be placed? Please tell us by directing the smoke of the incense.” Then the smoke went in the direction of Caoxi. So, on the thirteenth day of that month, along with his robe and bowl, the enshrined body was transported back. Next year, on the twenty-fifth day of the seventh lunar month, the body was taken out of the shrine and plastered with incense paste by his disciple Fangbian.

门人忆念取首之记，遂先以铁叶漆布，固护师颈入塔。忽于塔内，白光出现，直上冲天，三日始散。

In case that the head would be stolen as predicted by the Master, the disciples braced the neck with iron sheets covered by lacquered cloths before placing the body in the stupa. Suddenly, a white light appeared in the stupa, shot to the sky and lingered for three days before fading away.

韶州奏闻，奉敕立碑，纪师道行。师春秋七十有六，年二十四传衣，三十九祝发，说法利生三十七载。嗣法四十三人，悟道超凡者，莫知其数。达摩所传信衣，中宗赐磨衲宝钵，及方辩塑师真相，并道具等，永镇宝林道场。流传《坛经》，以显宗旨，兴隆三宝，普利群生者。

After [the official of] Shaozhou reported this to the court, the emperor ordered a monument to be established for the Master. The inscription on the monument reads: The Master, who passed away at the age of seventy-six, received the robe at the age of twenty-four, got ordained at thirty-nine, and taught Dharma for thirty-seven years. Among his followers, forty-three carried on his teaching and those who got enlightened are countless. His personal belongings—the robe from Bodhidharma, the bowl and the robe bestowed by the emperor, the sculpture of the Master made by Venerable Fangbian and other stuff—are kept in Baolin Temple. From hand to hand, *The Platform Sutra* (the essence of the Master's teaching) will reveal the essence of Chan, make Triple Gem shine, and bring benefits to sentient beings.